Peace through

Positive

Pass

People

it

Power!

On!

Jim Gentil

Compiled & Edited By Jim Gentil

Positive People Power!

Copyright 2001, Jim Gentil

Library of Congress Cataloging in Publication Data

Published by: Insight Publishing Company
P.O. Box 4189
Sevierville, TN 37864
Printed in the USA

Cover Design: Douglas Graphics, Sevierville, TN

ISBN No. 1-885640-70-6

Positive People Power

Table of Contents

Positive
People
Power!

Welcome to the your Personal World of Positive People Power!

With the information in this book you will be able to create your own:

Inspirational Insights
Motivational Moments
Positive Prototypes
Success Scenes
Fantastic Frames of Mind
Great Gulps of Gusto
Excellent Examples of Enthusiasm
Terrific Touchstones
Wonderful Words

Positive People Power

This book, Positive People Power! is a compilation of positive material designed to inspire you to fire your desire with enthusiasm to make your life productive and fill it with an abundance of success, happiness and love.

This book is the first 100 issues of the Positive People Power! newsletter, with unpublished additional material. The newsletter is published weekly, via e-mail, for advocates of positive living. It's filled with bite size nuggets of inspiration that when read over and over will make you a better person by changing and charging you with a positive attitude.

You will find some stories and quotes that will become your favorties and hopefully they will help you prepare a positive course of action that will become a part of your living experience.

Life is so very short and we never know which day will be our last. So live each day in the fullest possible way and leave your personal legacy to those you love and cherish.

****

The material in this book has been collected over a long period of time. Many of the original sources are unknown to the compiler. The compiler wishes to acknowledge the original authors, whoever they may be, but has confidence that they would urge, with him, "Do not inquire as to who said what, but pay attention to what is said."

DEDICATIONS

To the most positive people in my life - my wife, Janie, who has supported me in all my endeavors. To my daughter, Janna and husband, Todd - my son, Jeff and wife, Christine - who are now living their own positive dreams.

To all my friends and acquaintances, who have been a part of my life and have been an inspiration to me.

To my departed parents who instilled in me two strong values of education and hard work.

To all the contributors of comments in the newsletter, both living and deceased, thank you for your thoughts, words and ideas for others to live by.

* To all the subscribers whose encouragement helped me to persevere to keep doing the newsletter and whose comments follow:

* To the writer of this newsletter - your stories have touched me, inspired me, and enlightened me but this one was extra special... . Your e-mails make my day! An appreciative receiver, Claudia Machell

* Jim: Today's newsletter was absolutely magnificent. Thank you for sending it. Jean Palmer Heck - Real-Impact Inc.

* Jim: I used your emergency kit listing and explanation to start our Assistant Governor's training session. Thanks for all your great ideas. Pat Derr, DGE 5870

Positive People Power

* Your latest newsletter was really great! Especially the "List" for kids.- Steve Payne

* Thanks for the newsletter. It is definitely a winner and comes right in time each week! -Lucy Phifer

* I want to thank you for all of your uplifting messages. They are wonderful and I enjoy them all. Sincerely, -Jeanette Leon

* Jim...absolutely your **best** newsletter yet! I'm glad to be on your distribution list. Thank you. -Tom Britton. - Britton & Britton - Houston, TX

* Thank you Jim for the inspiring story of the mother bird. I truly enjoy your newsletter each week. Thank you so much for sharing it with all. -Becky O'Neill

* Man. I love and enjoy this more than the sermons I preach. What positive and solid "stuff". I hope that you were able to see the bio show on Norman V. Peale recently on TV. What a positive person who had many reasons not to be. If I could be like that. Jim-bo keep it up and include me. -Tom Carroll, pastor, Lakeway Ecumencial Church

* Jim, God Bless You. Thanx for the "bird Story". You are making a difference. For YOUR SUCCESS! -George

* Jim, Thanks for providing this newsletter. I enjoy reading it. It is a great way to start the day. Keep up the good work.
-Bob Eskridge, Austin, TX

Positive People Power

* Hey Jim: I just read your newsletter about the guy who packed Plumb's parachute. I've changed my mind. I don't want to be taken off of your list. I'd like to continue receiving your newsletter. I'm sort of going through a lot right now. In particular, I've had to close my business and look for a job. These are real trying times for me. I really got a lot out of your letter. I think I sort of need inspiring words right now. Funny how things work that way. Thanks again, -Rich.

* I wanted to thank you for your newsletter. It always seems to come just when I need it most. Take care, Dori Thornhill

* Jim: Just wanted to tell you, "THANKS FOR CONTINUING TO SEND ME THE POWERFUL NEWSLETTER, "Positive People Power." Keep It UP! - Glenn Altwein

* Jim, Congrats on your one year PPP Newsletter anniversary. It's always a joy to read and I have used several pieces to post on bulletin boards or fwd to friends.
Keep'em comin'! Peace, Bill Johnson

* I am a plant manager of a chemical plant in Deer Park, Texas and I share the Newsletter with all plant employees. The Newsletter is a tremendous tool in helping develop the kind of culture we want at our plant. Many employees give me positive feedback and they make hard copies and take them home. Even some may be using them in Sunday School classes. So, you get an A+ from our view point. Thanks a million for sharing it with us. (Name withheld)

* Thank you so much for the light you provide to the world and my soul. Every little bit counts and just that bit more may turn a

soul ever so gently toward the balance of love in their life and to all around them. Peace, Love , Light In the New Year and many more to come. -James Ochoa

* Hi Jim!! Just a note to tell you that I DO enjoy your newsletter soooooo much! It's with a smile I open each edition for that pearl of wisdom that I will use on any day, at the appropriate moment! JanaLee - Alexandria, VA

* Thank you for your timely newsletter. I have just discovered that my sales territory is changing and I was angry that opportunities which I have been working on for two years would no longer be my responsibility. I realize now that I have been "coasting", not having to scramble to do well. It has been a long time since I have been truly challenged, and this will give me the opportunity to stretch my skills. This could be the jumpstart that re-energizes my career. -Ed

* Thank you! That was so beautiful it gave me chills! I'm going to pass it on! -Jenny Sinex

* I personally want to thank you for sending us these newsletters they are very inspiring and definetly a booster, and they also keep hope alive. thanks (smile) -Sean Allen

* Just wanted to say "Thank You" for all you do.
I don't know how I was put on your list, but I have certainly been inspired by your letters. Hope the new year will bring you "Ten Thousand Joys and Blessings" as you continue to share positive messages. With best wishes, Eun Y. Kim

Positive People Power

* I receive many electronic newsletters from a variety of sources, but yours is by far the one that I am most anxious to read. You stand for something incredibly important! I just wanted to take a moment to say thank you for this wonderful gift.
Please continue to write, your words are very inspiring.
Adele Lynn - Lynn Learning Labs - Belle Vernon, PA

* Jim: Just wanted to say thanks for your continued good work in putting out the newsletter. Hope all is well with you....Sonny DiFranco- The Mac Guru

* Jim, I thoroughly enjoyed "Sixty Second System of Success". I have just read it for the first time and will peruse it more slowly next reading with the idea of following the instructions, specially the practice of starting off the day in a cheerful way. I'm convinced you are right. Now here is my comment: "Somehere during, after or before those four 15 second segments, I think we should thank God for helping us every day for his help as we go about all of our tasks, including this one".
You have probably covered this elsewhere, but I just wanted to mention this since you asked for comments. Don't get me wrong, I don't spend a lot of time on my knees, but I have noticed it seems to help me stay motivated and try harder to do my part when I do remember to thank God for doing his part. At any rate Jim, I really enjoyed your book and I'm looking forward to the other one. Thanks for all your writings. H. Motley

* There are days when your newsletter is just what I need to keep focused on the important things in life. I also like to share it with others when I know they are in need of inspiration. Thank you, Ginny Karul SC Johnson, Home Storage RD&E - Racine, WI

ix

Positive People Power

* I have so enjoyed my subscription to Positive People Power!
I have forwarded nearly every issue to someone. I print each issue
and put in a binder for future reference. I have used many of the
stories and quotes in presentations, meetings, trainings....
There is something in each issue that supports my mission of
helping others discover their "path"! Thank you for providing such
a quality newsletter! Cynthia Schiebel -Director of
Guidance/Health Services - Eanes ISD - Austin, TX

* Hello Jim, I have occasionally responded to your news letter
with great support. I pass them along to my employees. Some are
now even on your distribution list. I wanted to pass along a quote
from my wife that she said off the top of her head a couple years
ago when we were doing some business planning and goal setting.
"The only goal that is unattainable, is a goal that hasn't been set"
- Nancy McEvilly-Morrison
Thought I would pass it along for others to use and I also totally
believe in that simple phrase. It's simple fundamentals like that
that have made my company the fastest growing privately held
office supply company in central Texas over the past five years.
We will soon be the largest privately held office supply company
servicing Austin and surrounding communities. We're currently
#2 and fast approaching the #1 "privately held" spot. We'll raise
the bar again once we get there (#1 spot). "There are no secrets to
success, just fundamentals" Keep up the good work and positive
thoughts! P.D. Morrison - President/CEO-Hurricane Office Supply

* "Jim's presence in our lives truly makes the world a better place."
In this fast-paced, high-tech world in which we live, his pearls of
wisdom truly inspire us to live each day to the fullest....and remind
us to find beauty in the simple things in life that make it so worth
living!" - Barry J. Izsak, Arranging It All - Austin TX

x

Positive People Power

* This newsletter is just one of its editor's many gifts to humanity. It, and he, are always uplifting, kind and true. I have been blessed to personally know Jim, and he is just as sincere, positive and upbeat as his newsletter would imply. He and his newsletter have been an inspiration to me and have had a major impact on my life - as well as many other lives to whom I have passed on his kind words. -Cindy Suggs - APR - Houston, TX

* Dear Jim, We so much enjoy these Positive Power Newsletters! Sometimes, the message is just what I need for my day, and often find myself "waiting" for the next one.
Most sincerely, - Deborah Davidson

* Thank you for being my friend and chosen family. As I am never alone neither are you. Thank you, be well and know you're thought of even when I don't write. -Ruth Angel Marie

* Thank you for your words of wisdom, encouragement, insight and courage. I don't have a computer at home, but use the e-mail at work, and find your weekly publications inspiring. I'm not sure how you got my name, but thanks to you and whoever is out there watching over me. Heidi Radke - Albuquerque, NM

* Jim G...Thank you so much for including me in your positive people power newsletter. I look forward to every segment. It is truly thought provoking and inspiring! Don't forget me!
- K Garwick

* Please put me on your email list..I was sent this by a friend I don't see often who couldn't have known that at this time I really needed some positive thinking power. Thank u -Linda

Positive People Power

* Thanks for the newsletter this week. It's an especially challenging week. To write VICTORY next to each accomplishment, fuels my desire to complete the many tasks still ahead of me. Much more inspiring than crossing them off the list! - Erin

* Hi Jim! How are you? This newsletter was a good one! Thank You!! Am working at a Christian School now and am awed at how God is working. The theme of character is so appropriate. Bless you! Harriet

* I wanted to take just a minute to tell you how much I enjoy your newsletters. I don't always get to read them when they arrive but always make it a point to catch up later. Keep it up. Hope all is well with you and yours. - Chris

* I love how I feel when I read this publication. My first thought is to share it with as many people as I can. Dawna Thorstad - Astronaut Hall of Fame - Titusville, FL

* Great idea to send Thanksgiving letters! While I'm at it... you and Janie made a great impact on my life back in 1972 when I was a young graduate from high school and just on the brink of independence... you taught me how to be myself and how to have fun... and you respected me for my talents and made me feel like I was okay. Thanks for that and more!!! As I went through times of turmoil I often thought of the example of your relationship with one another and wished that I could have such a marital relationship. I now have a wonderful husband who loves me more than anyone deserves to be loved. He is such a blessing! ... Don't get me wrong.. he's not perfect! (hee! hee!) ....anyway, thanks for

all you did for me in that moment of my life! I am so glad that we are back in touch! Love, Theresa

* Dear Jim - I always enjoy your messages, but today's was special. I hope it inspires many of your readers to write such letters. It brings up the subject of thanking people via a note. I have always felt it important to sit down and send a few words to anyone who has done something special for me, or send a clipping I've seen about someone in the paper, along with a congratulatory note, etc. For four years I served as Supervisor of Maine Township, one of the largest townships in Illinois, and my staff received notes of appreciation from me on a regular basis. I didn't think much about this - just did it. I left office in 1993 and whenever I meet one of my staff at the store, or elsewhere, they rarely fail to tell me how they miss my notes of thanks. Anyway, I continue to take a few moments whenever I have an opportunity. It makes me feel better, and if the recipient feels good, too, so much the better. Thanks for your comments. Joan Hall

* I have been receiving the attached newsletter for about a year now. Many times I will pick out my favorite item and pass it on to you. Today I was reading this and decided I would send it to all of you. "IF" you want to receive this FREE newsletter please respond to the address at the bottom and Jim will add you to his list as well. Just because I send you something I like there may be something else in the letter that is meant for you. Jim sends this out every week. This has helped me to focus on the positive and I would wish this for my friends as well. SO-O-O if you want to receive this let Jim know. I hope you enjoy it as much as I do.
Judy Foster
PS: Thanks so much Jim - Keep up the GOOD positive work.

Positive People Power

* Great messages. Thanks for sharing and caring,
Perry A~ - Perry Productions - Austin, TX

* Jim - just wanted to let you know how much I enjoy your
newsletters! I look forward to hearing from you each week! Keep
up the good work and thanks for the inspiration! I share it with all
of my friends and family! :) gina

* Dad- Todd forwarded your latest newsletter to Sara Hickman,
and this is what she wrote back to him.....
Dear Todd...Wow...thank you so much for sharing this story...of
course, I was in tears...very moving... I also cried (of course-I am
my father's daughter!!)-thanks for the great story. love u Janna

* Thank you so very much for sending these messages to me. I
thoroughly enjoy them. I teach second grade and have often
thought about reading some of them to my students. They send
such a wonderful message. I appreciate you sending them to me.
Helen Dawkins

* What a beautiful story, and it came at a time that I have been
sitting around feeling sorry for myself because of what I didn't
have, rather than cherishing the blessings in my life. Thank you,
Jim, for helping to put things into perspective and "joy" into the
lives of others. Sue Merritt-Teacher - Brazosport Independent
School District

* Jim I just wanted to let you know how much I enjoy your
weekly newsletter and have been touched by exactly what I need
each time. Thank you, Sheryl

Positive People Power

* Mr. Jim Gentil, I just wanted to thank you for the wonderful newsletter I get every week. They always come when I need them most! I feel so inspired and good about myself when I follow through with your suggestions. THANKS!!
Have a happy day! tina ferderer

* Thank you so very much for the Positive People Power! Newsletter. I forward it to selected individuals and get very positive feedback. -Roy Coleman - MTTC - Louisville, KY

* Thanks so much for this message. I am going through a difficult time in my life right now because my husband doesn't know if he wants to be married anymore. Your message gave me hope and of course if things don't work out--I will be strong enough to get on with my life and help my daughter grow into the best young woman she can be. Thanks again--I really appreciate your messages....They are very uplifting... Kim

* Jim, thanks again for another inspirational "fix". I just loved it!
Shirley Markley - Shirley Markley Productions - Austin TX

* Dear Jim -Just want to tell you how I look forward to your messages. Today, your "worry" portion is especially applicable as I find myself sorting some challenges out.
Keep up the good work. Joan Hall

* Dear Jim Gentil, I enjoy your 'Positive Winners' email. Much appreciation for sending to my address. Patricia Pummel - Speakers Plus, Inc. - Rapid City, SD

* Jim -- Thanks for the newsletter! I'm impressed you got me in the system so quickly -- just like magic, huh! Speaking of magic, I thoroughly enjoyed your session last Friday. It was good to see you again. Thanks for putting me on your newsletter list. I thoroughly enjoyed reading it and look forward to receiving others. Have a wonderful week! -Marilyn M. Monroe - CAE

* Mr. Gentil, Thanks for your newsletters; I love them. They really do motivate me. Have a great week. -Gray Hardaway - Author

* Hey Jim, I was forwarded a copy of your newsletter from a friend of mine. I really enjoyed reading it and would like more in the future. Please add me to your mailing list.
Thanks! Reagan Knowles

* LOVE your newsletter...Keep up the Great Work....can I give you some of my friends' email names to have them on distribution list? If I could share your thoughts and energy with others..I would like to share your messages. Working Warrior, .. Kirk Farber

*You really nailed the Valentines Day spirit with the latest one. We have such big dreams that sometimes J and I get caught up in trying to acheive them rather than enjoying the journey towards them. THANKS for reminding me! Love, Todd

If you would like to receive the Positive People Power! Newsletter weekly, reply with "SUBSCRIBE" in the subject line to: StartRight@aol.com. This mailing list is never revealed to anyone for any purpose.

Power
Points

**"It's a funny thing about life;
if you refuse to accept
anything but the best,
you very often get it."
-W. Somerset Maugham**

A person's attitude is one of the fundamental determinants of success. The rudiments of success are to be found in the mind. It is a principle written in Scripture. "As a man thinketh in his heart, so is he." These words from King Solomon, found in Chapter 23, Verse 7 of Proverbs, make the same point as Earl Nightingale, "you become what you think about!" Ralph Waldo Emerson updated the philosophy, "A man is what he thinks about all day long." And John Miller further modernized the concept, "The way we think determines happiness. It doesn't depend upon who you are or what you have; it depends solely upon what you think."

Think about what you think, for it provides a mirror to the world of your heart and soul.

If you <u>think </u>you are beaten, you are.
If you <u>think</u> you dare not, you don't.
If you like to win, but <u>think</u> you can't,
It's almost certain you won't.

If you <u>think</u> you'll lose, you've lost,
For out of this world we find
Success begins with a person's will,
It's all in our <u>state of mind</u>.

If you <u>think</u> you're outclassed, you are.
You've got to <u>think </u>high to rise.
You've got to <u>be sure of yourself</u> before
You can ever win a prize.

Cause life's battles don't always go
To the stronger or faster man,
But sooner or later, the person who wins
Is the person WHO THINKS HE CAN.

The four keys to developing persistence and purpose
1. Rekindle and refire your vision and purpose everyday. Draw daily inspiration from the rewards you will receive when your vision is realized.
2. Anchor the following attitude deep within your mind and heart. "I can achieve anything I set my mind to, no matter how much hard work it takes, no matter how difficult it is, no matter how long it takes. I can and will achieve it."
3. Realize that obstacles and setbacks will be set on your pathway as you strive to attain your vision and purpose. Realize that these difficulties are really opportunities from which you can learn new insights that will strengthen your resolve and increase your knowledge.
4. Turn your work into fun. Make what you have to do something you want to do.

Failure is failure only if you fail to learn from it.

With the beginning of a new year, many of us have resolutions to go on a diet and to become more physically fit. For those who really want to - you will do it. For those who just think they want to - we offer this tongue-in-cheek diet.

Dieting Under Stress

<u>This diet is designed to help you cope with the stress that builds up during the day</u>

Breakfast

8 oz. nonfat (skim) milk
1 bowl oatmeal with 1 tsp. brown sugar
1 piece whole wheat toast

Lunch

4 oz. broiled chicken breast (remove skin before eating)
5 cherry tomatoes
1/2 cup steamed baby carrots
1 orange or apple
1 Oreo cookie
Herb tea

After-work snack

Rest of the package of Oreos
1 quart Rocky Road ice cream
1 jar hot fudge

Dinner

1 large extra cheese and pepperoni pizza
1 loaf buttered garlic bread
1 large pitcher of beer
3 Milky Ways
Entire frozen cheesecake (eaten directly from freezer)

You never work for somebody else. Someone else might sign your check but you're the one who fills in the amount. - Anonymous

Tact is the ability to stay in the middle without getting caught there.
- Franklin P. Jones

A survey of women graduates of prominent women's colleges showed an average of 3.7 children per graduate. A similar survey of men's schools showed an average of 2.4 children per graduate. The conclusion from these figures is apparent...women have more children than men.

See things as you would have them be - instead of as they are.
- Robert Collier

A study conducted by the Harvard Business School found that individuals with written, clearly defined goals obtain higher levels of achievement than those without goals. The study found:
* 83 % of the population does not have goals.
* 14 % had specific goals but weren't written.
* The 14 % earned 3 times what the other 83 % did.
* 3 % had written goals.
Those 3 % earned 10 times what the 83 % did.
There is unlimited power in written goals!

THE SIX "MUSTS" OF SUCCESS!
1. You "must" have a specific goal.
2. You "must" have a specific time to achieve your goal.
3. You "must" write it down.
4. You "must" develop a plan to achieve your goal.
5. You "must" decide what kind of price you're willing to pay.
6. You "must" think about reaching your goal everyday.

If you could live your life over, what would you do differently and why?
Whatever you come up with, write that down!
That becomes your goal!
Now why haven't you achieved that and what do you need to do to achieve it?
Answer these questions and you are on your way to establishing your goals!

Goals enable us to control the direction of change in our lives.

Be careful what you say about your goals. If you say I'm almost there - you'll always be almost there. When you get there, you'll know it and you'll know it's time to set new and bigger goals.

If it's getting easier - you ain't climbing!

Think of this: The human being is the only creature in the universe that has the capacity of exercising creative imagination. This divine quality of dreaming what you want to be, where you want to go, what you'd love to do, projects you hope to achieve, goals you'd like to reach - all of this makes you human and the most unique creature in all of creation!!!

SPELL CHECKER
I have a spelling checker.
It came with my PC;
It plainly marks for my revue
Mistakes I cannot sea.

Positive People Power

I've run this pome threw it,
I'm sure your pleas to no,
Its letter perfect in it's weigh,
My checker tolled me sew.

General Colin Powell's Rules

Some " thoughts to live by" that the general has collected over the years.

1.   It ain't as bad as you think. It will look better in the morning.
2.   Get mad, then get over it.
3.   Avoid having your ego so close to your position that when your position falls your ego goes with it.
4.   It can be done!
5.   Be careful what you choose, you may get it.
6.   Don't let adverse facts stand in the way of a good decision.
7.   You can't make someone else's choices. You shouldn't let someone else make yours.
8.   Check small things.
9.   Share credit.
10. Remain calm. Be kind.
11. Have a vision.
12. Don't take counsel of your fears or naysayers.
13. Perpetual optimism is a force multiplier.

The quality of a person's life is in direct proportion to his or her commitment to personal excellence.

GOAL SETTING SUCCESS STEPS
1.	Must have desire.
2.	Must be attainable.
3.	Write it out in detail.
4.	Determine benefits.
5.	Analyze where you are now to measure base point.
6.	Set deadlines.
7.	Identify obstacles.
8.	Clearly define knowledge necessary to obtain goals.
9.	Identify people, groups, organizations needed to help me attain goal.
10.	Write plan - all necessary activities and prioritize. Review and rewrite as often as necessary. Write in present tense terms as if already achieved.
11.	Visualize clear picture of goal achieved and replay as often as possible.
12.	Back your plan with determination, resolve and persistence to never give up.

Let's talk about Affirmations! In fact, let's talk to ourselves!

WE BECOME WHAT WE THINK ABOUT! and by telling ourselves positive affirmations we will become what we think about.

Do you want to change your attitude from a run-of-the-mill person bordering on being a couch-potato to one of vibrant self-esteem? or...Do you want to stretch your already enthusiastic personality to even greater heights? Then start your day in a positive way using POWER affirmations.

By giving yourself POWER affirmations the first thing in the morning, you are setting yourself up for a positive day. Tests show that the first person you meet each day has more effect on your mood than the next five people you meet. So you be the first person you meet each day and meet yourself with POWER affirmations.

I believe that we need to always tell ourselves the positives about ourselves. <u>We don't need to tell ourselves negatives, other people will take care of that for us</u>. So, when you wake up in the morning, look in the mirror, put a smile on your face and repeat the following POWER affirmations.

I FEEL FANTASTIC, I FEEL GREAT,
I FEEL SUPER, I FEEL TERRIFIC, I FEEL WONDERFUL.
I'M NUMBER ONE, I LIKE MYSELF, I LOVE MYSELF,
I'M AT PEACE WITH MYSELF.
I'M THE BEST, I'M THE GREATEST
AND THIS DAY I'M ACHIEVING MY GOAL,
BECAUSE I'M A POSITIVE POWERED WINNER,
AND WINNERS SAY "**YES!**"

Do this and you will set the mood and the tone for the kind of day you want to have. When someone asks me, "How are you doing?" I always say "Fantastic" and I say it enthusiastically. This does two things: <u>One</u>, it makes me feel better because I've told myself a positive affirmation and <u>two</u>, I've committed myself to being fantastic. The other person expects me to be and feel fantastic because I said I was, so consequently, I must act that way. It's the self-fulfilling prophecy. If others perceive us to be enthusiastic, we will continue to act out those perceptions, because perception is reality.

<u>SAY IT - FEEL IT - ACT IT - AND YOU WILL BE IT.</u>
From: *The Sixty Second System of Success* by Jim Gentil.

"What you believe is what you achieve and when you know clearly what you want, you'll wake up every morning excited about life." - Mark Victor Hansen

Opposites attract, because that's the way God wanted it. God never put two people alike together, because if He did, one would then be obsolete.

NOTICE:
TO MAKE THINGS EASIER FOR ALL OF US, PLEASE NOTICE THIS IMPORTANT NOTICE ABOUT NOTICES.
YOU MAY HAVE NOTICED THE INCREASED AMOUNT OF NOTICES FOR YOU TO NOTICE.
WE NOTICE THAT SOME OF OUR NOTICES HAVE NOT BEEN NOTICED. THIS IS VERY NOTICEABLE!
IT HAS BEEN NOTICED THAT THE RESPONSES TO THE NOTICES HAVE BEEN NOTICEABLY UNNOTICEABLE.

Positive People Power

THIS NOTICE IS TO REMIND YOU TO NOTICE THE NOTICES AND RESPOND TO THE NOTICES BECAUSE WE DO NOT WANT THE NOTICES TO GO UNNOTICED.

NOTICE COMMITTEE FOR NOTICING NOTICES

One of man's greatest desires in life is to find someone who will make him do what he is capable of doing. - Emerson

If you want happiness...
For an hour - take a nap
For a day - go fishing
For a month - take a trip
For a year - inherit a fortune
For a lifetime - help someone else - Chinese Proverb

EXPECT THE BEST
What's exciting about life is that every morning offers a brand-new day with unlimited possibilities. Yesterday's mistakes and regrets belong to yesterday. Today is a clean slate, a chance to start over, to do or become anything you want, a chance to go for it! So, jump into life with both feet! Go forward, head held high, expecting the best...you may be surprised at how often that's exactly what you'll get.

Some ideas on visualizing success in your life.
T.V. Station of the Mind
Along with the thousands of words running through our minds, there are thousands of pictures. The orderly control of these pictures is called imaging, imagineering, visioneering or positive realization.

Having and using your Attitude of Positive Expectancy will help you achieve your goals. We program our personal TV stations everyday through the active use of our imagination. Because we are in control, we can program positively and we can deliberately imagine new expectations for ourselves. All we have to do is to imagine ourselves winning, being happy, having goods days, and seeing the opportunity in every difficulty which may come our way. Remember, WINNERS SEE WHAT THEY WANT and they always want to win.

The Human Brain is the fastest working, coolest running, most compact and efficient computer mechanism ever produced in large quantities by unskilled labor.

THAWLEY'S LAW: There is no notion, no theory, no concept so absurd, that it can't fill an auditorium in California.

We might have to be careful about what we visualize, for it may have some devastating effect, as the following story illustrates.
A middle-aged woman has a heart attack and is taken to the hospital. While on the operating table she has a near-death experience. During that experience she sees God and asks if this is it? God say no and explains that she has another 30-40 years to live.
Upon her recovery she decides to just stay in the hospital and have a face lift, liposuction, breast augmentation, tummy tuck, etc. She even has someone come in and change her hair color. She figures since she's got another 30-40 years she might as well make the most of it. She walks out of the hospital after the last operation and is killed by an ambulance speeding up to the hospital.

She arrives in front of God and asks, "I thought you said I had another 30-40 years?"
God replies, "I didn't recognize you!"

A good listener is not only popular everywhere, but after a while he knows something. - Wilson Mizner

Let's talk about Networking as it relates to improving your business! An old technique I learned (from where I don't know) is to use a mental picture of a house as a means of creating or extending conversation and finding out more about your customer. When you meet someone and the conversation starts to drag after the introduction, visualize a house and use that as a prompt to easily converse with anyone.

HOUSE - where do you live? what area of the city? what neighborhood? are you married? do you have children? what school district? what activities or sports are your kids involved in?

LIVING ROOM - what do you do to relax? what's your favorite TV show or movie? do you like to travel? where have you been? what is your favorite place to visit or you would like to visit?

KITCHEN - what kinds of food do you like? do you have a favorite restaurant? know any good recipes? ever have anything unusual happen to you in a restaurant?

FAMILY ROOM - what activities are you involved in - clubs, organizations, etc.? do you have other family members living in the area? do you ever have a family reunion?

YARD - do you have pets? do you like flowers, yardwork, etc.?

GARAGE - what kind of car do you have? do you like fishing, hunting, woodworking or any other outdoor activity?

I'm sure you can come up with more questions to ask by visualizing the house and what it means to you and what you think it may mean to your customer or new found friend. If you use this technique and do it with sincerity you will know more about your customer/friend and you will be able to serve them more effectively.

A DAY OFF
So you want the day off.
Let's take a look at what you are asking for.
There are 365 days per year available for work.
There are 52 weeks per year in which you already have two days off per week, leaving 261 days available for work.
Since you spend 16 hours each day away from work, you have used up 170 days, leaving only 91 days available for work.
You spend 30 minutes each day on coffee break that accounts for 23 days each year, leaving only 68 days available for work.
With a one hour lunch period each day, you have used up another 46 days, leaving only 22 days available for work.
You normally spend 2 days per year on sick leave. This leaves you only 20 days available for work.
We are off 5 holidays per year, so your available working time is down to 15 days.

We generously give you 14 days vacation per year, which leaves only 1 day available for work...
So there's no way I'm going to give you the day off!!!

Put these ideas into action this week:
1. Focus on each person you're speaking with today. Practice your listening skills.
2. Ask a young person's opinion and truly listen to the answer.
3. Help lift another person's spirits, silently, through prayer.
4. Praise a child in front of his or her parents, grandparents, or teachers.
5. Share your heart with everyone you meet.

Most all of us are endowed with the five senses...maybe they don't all work too well...but, most of us can see - hear - smell - touch and taste........but what we all really need (if we don't have it) is the sixth sense.......a sense of humor to give us a terrific outlook on life.

A true sense of humor is where you laugh at yourself with others rather than laugh at others with others.

The sixth sense helps you to relieve stress, reduce tension, gives you a good self-image, increases your self-esteem, exercises your insides, and makes you feel good all over.

A sense of humor will help you over life's hurdles better than any medicine or drug. Laughter is the greatest tonic in the world and it's my drug of choice...and it is kind of like a drug, because laughter releases endorphins which are pain relievers and stress reducers.

To be successful in whatever business you're in, you've got to STP - see the people. You've got to go out and show your smiling face to them. And if you don't have a smiling face....then as a college Prof. of mine once said.....if you don't have a smile and a sense of humor then you better go out and beg, borrow or steal one...because nothing will help you to succeed more in life than a sense of humor and a smile on your face. You should never leave the house without this important part of make-up on your face.

Learn to laugh often! Because laughter is just about the best medicine known. Medical science is beginning to research the effects that laughter has upon people's health and have found plenty to smile about. Studies have revealed that a good belly laugh will help fight infections, stress, hypertension and headaches. A hearty laugh will stimulate your chest, diaphragm, heart, lungs and liver. Your pulse can shoot from 60 to 120 as your blood pressure rises from 120 to 200 as an increased supply of oxygen courses through your bloodstream. Laughter affects blood pressure both ways. If you have low blood pressure, laughter will raise it. If it's high, laughter will put it back down where it belongs. In this age of high-tech, scientific miracles and medical break-throughs, it just might be that something as simple as laughter is the best medicine - really. So have a good laugh whenever and wherever the mood strikes you.

THOUGHTS TO GET YOU THROUGH ALMOST ANY CRISIS

* Indecision is the key to flexibility.
* If you ever find something you like, buy a lifetime supply because they will stop making it.
* You can't tell which way the train went by looking at the track.
* Be kind, everyone you meet is fighting a tough battle.
* There is absolutely no substitute for a genuine lack of preparation.
* By the time you make ends meet, they move the ends.
* Nostalgia isn't what it used to be.
* Sometimes too much to drink isn't enough.
* The world gets a little better each day...and worse in the evening.
* Not one shred of evidence exist in favor of the idea that life is serious.
* Someone who thinks logically is a nice contrast to the real world.
* Things are more like they are today than they have ever been before.
* The other line always moves faster until you get in it.
* Everything should be made as simple as possible, but no simpler.
* It's hard to be nostalgic when you can't remember anything.
* One seventh of your life is spent on Monday.

Have a Fantastic Week! and put these ideas into action this week:
1. Resolve to live your life with less judgment and more compassion, less fear and more faith.
2. Instead of a quick hello, spend an extra minute to really connect with someone today.
3. Do something especially kind for yourself today.

3. Do something especially kind for yourself today.
4. Be extra courteous when driving.
5. Share an inspiring quote with your co-workers and loved ones.

There are only two ways to live your life. One is as though nothing is a miracle. The other is as though everything is a miracle.
 - Albert Einstein

When everything seems to be going against you, remember the airplane takes off against the wind, not with it. -Henry Ford

SOME OF LIFE'S MOST IMPORTANT LESSONS
If you open it, close it.
If you turn it on, turn it off.
If you unlock it, lock it.
If you break it, fix it.
If you can't fix it, call someone who can.
If you borrow it, return it.
If you use it, take care of it.
If you make a mess, clean it up.
If you move it, put it back.
If you drop it, pick it up.
If you sleep on it, make it up.
If you empty it, fill it.
If it rings, answer it.
If it barks or meows, feed it.
If it cries, love it.
If it belongs to somebody else, get permission to use it.

If you don't know how to operate it, leave it alone.
If it doesn't concern you, don't mess with it.

Another of Life's Lessons

There was a little boy with a bad temper. His father gave him a bag of nails and told him that every time he lost his temper, to hammer a nail in the back fence.

The first day the boy had driven 37 nails into the fence. Then it gradually dwindled down. He discovered it was easier to hold his temper than to drive those nails into the fence.

Finally the day came when the boy didn't lose his temper at all. He told his father about it and the father suggested that the boy now pull out one nail for each day that he was able to hold his temper.

The days passed and the young boy was finally able to tell his father that all the nails were gone. The father took his son by the hand and led him to the fence. "You have done well, my son, but look at the holes in the fence. The fence will never be the same. When you say things in anger, they leave a scar just like this one. You can put a knife in a man and draw it out, it won't matter how many times you say 'I'm sorry,' the wound is still there. A verbal wound is as bad as a physical one."

A preacher found three boys playing hooky from school. "Don't you want to go to heaven?" asked the preacher? "Sure do," two of the boys answered. But the third one replied, "No, siree!" The preacher, surprised, asked again. "Don't you want to go to heaven when you die?" The boy let out a sigh of relief, "Oh, when I die? Of course, I do. I thought you were getting up a group to go now."

Take things as they come. But try to make things come as you would like to take them. - Curt Green

Parents never fully appreciate teachers unless it rains all weekend. - Bob Goddard

Put these ideas into action:
1. Hide a love note where you know someone will find it.
2. Say a prayer of thanks for your parents wherever they are.
3. Turn off the TV and have a conversation with someone in your family.
4. Spend ten minutes to make a list of things for which you are grateful. Remember them all day.
5. Exercise your waistline by picking up a few pieces of litter.

"Treat people as if they were what they ought to be and you help them become what they are capable of being." - Goethe

The knowledge that others believe in us and are counting on us acts as a self-fulfilling prophecy and helps us to become as good as they think we are. Leontyne Price, the great soprano, got her first job, as a maid, with a family who predicted that she had the making of a star - and made it a self-fulfilling prophecy by convincing Miss Price herself. When Roger Bannister began training to beat the four-minute mile, hardly anybody believed it could be done. "At first I wasn't quite sure either," said Bannister. "But I knew my trainer believed in me and I couldn't let him down." In business and industry, where the results of attitudes can be measured in dollars, experience has shown that it pays to overestimate, rather than underestimate, an employee's abilities. A good boss makes his people realize they have more ability than they think they have so that they consistently do better work than they thought they could. If you enlarge the opportunity, the person will expand to fill it.

CHILDREN LEARN WHAT THEY LIVE
by Dorothy Law Nolte
If a child lives with criticism,
He learns to condemn.
If a child lives with hostility,
He learns to fight.
If a child lives with ridicule,
He learns to be shy.
If a child lives with shame,
He learns to feel guilty.
If a child lives with tolerance,
He learns to be patient.
If a child lives with encouragement,
He learns confidence.
If a child lives with praise,
He learns to appreciate.
If a child lives with fairness,
He learns justice.
If a child lives with security,
He learns to have faith.
If a child lives with approval,
He learns to like himself.
If a child lives with acceptance and friendship,
He learns to find love in the world.

EXPECT THE BEST
What's exciting about life is that every morning offers a brand-new day with unlimited possibilities. Yesterday's mistakes and regrets belong to yesterday. Today is a clean slate, a chance to start over, to do or become anything you want, a chance to go for it! So, jump into life with both feet! Go forward, head held high, expecting the best...you may be surprised at how often that's exactly what you'll get.

AN OLD IRISH BLESSING
May the blessing of light be on you, light without and light within. And may the light shine out of your eyes like a candle set in the windows of a house, bidding the wanderer to come in out of the storm. And may the blessing of rain be on you - the soft sweet rain. May it fall upon your spirit so that all the little flowers may spring up, and shed their sweetness on the air. And may the blessing of the earth be on you - may you ever have a kindly greeting for them you pass as you're going along the roads. May the earth be soft under you when you rest out upon it, tired at the end of a day, and may it rest easy over you when, at the last, you lie out under it. May it rest so lightly over you that your soul may be off from under it quickly, and up and off, and on its way to God. And now may the Lord bless you, and bless you kindly.

When you have to make a choice and don't make it, that is in itself a choice. - William James

The best inheritance a parent can give to their children is a few minutes of their time each day. - O.A. Battista

ARE YOU A COMPLACENT PELICAN?
Some years ago flocks of pelicans were found starving on a California beach. Many dead ones littered the shore and created a severe problem for the Public Health Department.
Fishermen in this area were accustomed to cleaning their fish and discarding the refuse in shallow waters on their way to land. Nearby pelicans no longer had to work for their food. Lazily they became satisfied with what was tossed from fishing boats.
When Health Authorities for sanitary reasons prevented men from casting these cleanings in the water, the pelicans were without their easy daily supply.
Pelicans have a ladle-like bill which makes them excellent fishers, but these birds had become used to food without work. They had lived dully for so long they forgot how to strive. Unused to fending for their needs they began starving on the beach.
Then someone had a brilliant idea. Why not import a large group of energetic pelicans from Alaska and set them free on this California shoreline? As soon as the Alaskan birds were set down they quickly hurried into the water and began fishing. The sluggish ones watched. Gradually one by one they followed their ambitious friends until the whole colony was wading out and satisfying its hunger with scoopfuls of baby fish.
Do you allow your innate talents and inborn abilities to be starved out by existing off the unimaginative ideas of others? Like the pelican, nature has provided you with a marvelous mechanism, a creative brain, which when used efficiently makes life successful and infinitely wonderful. Associate with those who go after their goals

23

and soon you too will be wading out into greater depths of accomplishment.   - Ida F. Killian

There is an old saying: "When the student is ready, the teacher will appear." Like the pelicans we can be the mentors, teachers, personal trainers to those who are in need. We can also be the student in need of a teacher, who will help us learn new ways of doing things or relearn that which we have forgotten. Ask yourself which role should you be playing right now - mentor or student? or both? Take the time to focus on your strengths and pass them on or take time to learn more about your strong points!

Smiling and laughter can be seeds to succeeding. In fact, Ralph Waldo Emerson said just that in the opening lines of this verse about success:
To laugh often and love much,
To win the respect of intelligent people and the affection of children,
To earn the approbation of honest critics and endure the betrayal of false friends,
To appreciate beauty,
To give of ones' self,
To leave this world a bit better, whether by a healthy child, a garden patch, or a redeemed social condition,
To have played and laughed with enthusiasm and sung with exultation,
To know even one life has breathed easier because you have lived,
THIS IS TO HAVE SUCCEEDED!

Things to do this week:

1. Give thanks for your education. Seek ways to help others with their quest for knowledge.
2. Take an extra moment to think things through before acting.
3. Place a positive quote where someone will find it.
4. Revive a lost dream. Maybe now is the time to make it happen.
5. Be aware of every good thing that happens.

Always put off until tomorrow what you shouldn't do at all.
- Morris Mandel

It is part of the cure to wish to be cured. - Seneca

Freedom is no heritage. Preservation of freedom is a fresh challenge and a fresh conquest for each generation. It is based on the religious concept of the dignity of man. The discovery that man is free is the greatest discovery of the ages. - C. Donald Dallas

A characteristic of the positive-powered winner is a determination to do things rather than to talk about them. An examination of the things a positive-powered winner does, the way he works, tells a lot about him and that helps in distinguishing between those who get things done and those who don't.
1. He's always searching for opportunities all the time.
2. He's afraid of acting too late.
3. He's looking for ways to prevent failure.
4. He's actively exploring different courses of action.
5. He's willing to take risks.
6. He's determined to see projects through to the end.
7. He's repeating patterns of success that have proved productive for himself and others in the past.

This is the kind of thinking of a positive-powered winner and is found where the action is taking place.

A book is a success when people who haven't read it pretend they have. - Los Angeles Times Syndicate

We are only young once. That is all society can stand.
 - Bob Bowen

Four keys strategies to inspire employees to act:
1. Allow the freedom to fail and try again.
2. Create freedom from bureaucracy.
3. Encourage challenges to the status quo.
4. Give everyone input into firing troublesome customers.
 - Jim Harris - *Getting Employees to Fall in Love With Your Company*

There are three ways to get something done:
1. Do it yourself.
2. Hire someone to do it.
3. Forbid your kids to do it.
    - *I'm So Glad You Told Me What I Didn't Want to Hear*

The Eagle and the Rattlesnake
        There is a great battle that rages inside every person.
One side is the soaring eagle. Everything the eagle stands for is good and true and beautiful. The eagle soars high above the clouds. Even though it dips down into the valleys, the eagle builds its nest on the mountain tops.
        The other side is the slithering serpent, the rattlesnake.

That crafty, deceitful snake represents the worst aspects of a person - the darker side. The snake feeds upon one's downfalls and setbacks, and justifies itself by its presence in the slithering mass.

Who wins this great battle in your life? <u>None other than the one that is fed the most</u> - the eagle, or the rattlesnake. Who do feed the most?

Action items for this week
1. Give someone a surprise gift.
2. Make a funny home video with family members and send it to a relative.
3. Bring donuts to work, to teachers, to the nursing home, or police department.
4. Send a donation to a charity you've considered helping but haven't done so before.
5. Who do you know that needs a hug the most? Find a way to give it.

List on a piece of paper all the resources you need to achieve your desired goal.
Overlook nothing. Do you need more time or money, education or tools?
Make sure you've included everything.
Have you included on the list your own positive imagination, your faith?
What you imagine is what will transpire!
What you believe is what you will achieve!
Nothing is more important on that entire list than your own faith and imagination!
Think success and you'll achieve it!

If you must worry, do it right. Worry about only one thing at a time. Don't clutter up your mind fretting with numerous matters. This will fill your head with unnecessary junk. If you must worry, concentrate. Fix your mental powers on a single object. With a little effort, you may worry it to death, rather than permitting it to worry you to death. Follow the example of the clock.

The Clock That Had a Nervous Breakdown!
The clock was new and went about its business with precision of performing two ticks per second. Then something began to happen. It started thinking about all the ticks it was going to have to tick. The pressure of obligations created a maladjustment in the mainspring. The timepiece stayed awake fretting about its responsibilities. Two ticks to the second equals 120 ticks to the minute, which means 7200 ticks each hour and 172,800 ticks a day. In addition, it must tick 1,209,600 times per week for all fifty-two weeks of the year, or a grand total of 62,899,200 ticks annually.
The clock fell apart. Contemplating all those ticks caused a nervous breakdown. It was taken to a psychiatrist who went to work on the mainspring. The doctor asked, "Clock, what's your trouble?"
The clock looked up from the couch and told about all the ticking it had to do.
"Wait a minute," ordered the psychiatrist. "How many ticks do you have to tick at a time?"
"Oh," replied the clock, "I only have to tick one tick at a time."
"All right," prescribed the doctor, "you go home and tick only one tick at a time. Don't even think about the next tick until you get it ticked."

Twenty years have passed, and the clock is ticking right along, even now. That's the way to worry. Do it one tick at a time. - Ralph Phelps

The most successful people in the world never look for just a "job." They always figure some way they can be helpful to someone. And a lot of them hold positions created solely to make use of what they have to offer. - Dr. Irwin Ross

Every job is a self-portrait of the person who did it...autograph your work with excellence! - The Christian Reader

Positive Actions for the Week:
1. Pray for the world's leaders to make decisions with wisdom, courage and integrity.
2. Affirm your own goodness by giving thanks for all your special qualities.
3. Look your best - make an extra effort to shine. How does it make you feel?
4. Really be there for someone this week.
5. Go on an Easter Egg Hunt with some kids - yours or someone else's.

God asks no man whether he will accept life. That is not the choice. One must take it. The only choice is how.
- Henry Ward Beecher

Positive People Power

Inspirational
Insights

**"There are thousands of reasons
why you cannot do what you want to.
All you need is one reason why you can."
- Willis R. Whitney**

I'd like to share with you the story of two educationally handicapped children who knew what time was worth to them and who kept their diligence in spite of affliction.

The parents of the first child were not considered successful. His father was unemployed with no formal schooling. His mother was a teacher - and there was probably tension in the family because of this mismatch.

This child, born in Port Huron, Michigan, was estimated to have an IQ of 81. He was withdrawn from school after three months - and was considered backward by school officials.

Physically, the child enrolled two years late due to scarlet fever and respiratory infections. And he was going deaf. His emotional health was poor - stubborn, aloof, showing very little emotion.

He liked mechanics. He liked to play with fire and burned down his father's barn. He showed some manual dexterity, but used very poor grammar. But he did want to be a scientist and a railroad mechanic.

The second child was born of an alcoholic father who worked as an itinerant - a mother who stayed at home.

As a child, she was sickly, bedridden, and often hospitalized.

She was considered erratic and withdrawn. She would bite her nails and had numerous phobias. She wore a back brace from a spinal defect and would constantly seek attention.

She was a daydreamer with no vocational skills, although she expressed a desire to help the elderly and the poor.

Who were these children?

The boy from Port Huron became one of the world's greatest inventors, Thomas A. Edison.

And the awkward and sickly young girl, became a champion of the oppressed - Eleanor Roosevelt.

A diamond is a chunk of coal that made good under pressure.

"I long to accomplish great and noble tasks, but it is my chief duty to accomplish small tasks as if they were great and noble." -Helen Keller

In ancient times a king decided to find and honor the greatest person among his subjects. A man of wealth and property was singled out. Another was praised for her healing powers, another for his wisdom and knowledge of the law. Still another was lauded for his business acumen. Many other successful people were brought to the palace, and it became evident that the task of choosing the greatest would be difficult.

Finally, the last candidate stood before the king. It was a woman. Her hair was white. Her eyes shone with the light of knowledge, understanding and love.

"Who is this?" asked the king. "What has she done?"

"You have seen and heard all the others." said the king's aide.

"This is their teacher!"

The people applauded and the king came down from the throne to honor her. - Anonymous

Positive action items for the coming week:
1. Whenever the word "impossible" jumps into your head, drop the "im" and stay focused on the "possible."
2. Be ready to laugh at yourself.

3. Help someone else with a generous contribution of your special talents.
4. Start a new tradition. Find something to celebrate and make it a special day.
5. Do the project you've been dreading the most. Knock it off your list so you can forget about it.

The customer may not always be right, but he is right more often than he is wrong. Good customer service may be hard to define, but as someone once said, " I don't exactly know what good customer service is, but I know it when I receive it."

HERE ARE SOME TRUTHS ABOUT YOUR CUSTOMERS:
* They don't mind paying a lot of money for a product or service, just as long as the quality merits the price.

* They have a basic human need for security, dignity, self-respect and the respect of others. They are looking for a relationship of trust. The key to providing it, is the fact that you and/or your staff want to build this trust. Please underline the word "want" in your mind. If your employees aren't capable of wanting a warm customer relationship, perhaps they should be in the employ of someone else.

* They have emotions and intellects. They all have experiences as customers and buyers. They may also have experiences as sellers. They want you to be customer oriented, though they've probably never used or heard that phrase. They have, however, dealt with businesses that were or weren't customer oriented. They're aware of the difference.

* <u>They are not dependent on you. But you are dependent on them.</u>

34

* They are doing you a favor by giving you the opportunity to serve them. You are not doing them a favor by serving. They are not interruptions of your work. They are the purpose of your work.

* They are not outsiders to your business. Instead, they're a vital part of it. They keep it alive. The more you realize that, the healthier they'll keep your business and your bottom line.

* They are not people to argue with. Do you think your business could win an argument with a customer? You may win a skirmish but you will lose the war.

* They bring you their wants and needs. It is your job to fill and solve them. The better you do that job, the more profitable your business will be.

* They are the basis for most successful businesses in America - by their repeat business and their positive recommendations. Their withholding of repeat business and their negative recommendations are the basis of many failures.

* It all comes down to the Golden Rule: Treat customers as you would want to be treated if you were the customer.

You make a difference to your customers one at a time as this old story illustrates. An old man walked along the beach one morning at dawn and noticed a youth ahead of him picking up starfish and flinging them into the sea. Finally, catching up with the youth, he asked him why he was doing this. The answer was that the stranded starfish would die if left in the morning sun. "But the beach goes on

for miles and there are millions of starfish," countered the old man.
"How can your effort make any difference?"
The young man looked at the starfish in his hand and then threw it to
the safety of the waves. "It makes a difference to this one," he said.

Any relationship where you put yourself first won't last.
- Bill Copeland

When someone says, "That's a good question, "you can be sure it's
a lot better than the answer you're going to get."

What great things would you attempt if you knew you could not fail?

Patience is the ability to put up with people you'd like to put down.
- Ulrike Ruffert

Have you planted your spring garden yet? You might want to
consider planting the seeds for your garden of life.
First, Plant Five Rows of P's
Presence
Promptness
Preparation
Perseverance
Purity
Next, Plant Three Rows of Squash
Squash gossip
Squash indifference
Squash unjust criticism
Then Plant Five Rows of Lettuce
Let us be faithful to duty
Let us be unselfish and loyal

Positive People Power

Let us obey the rules and regulations
Let us be true to our obligations and
Let us love one another
No Garden is Complete Without Turnips
Turn up for meetings
Turn up with a smile
Turn up with new ideas
Turn up with determination to make everything count for
something good and worthwhile.
It would also be advisable to let our children play in this garden
and who knows what will grow out of that.

The best way to break a bad habit is to drop it. - Leo Aikman
The contest lasts for moments, though the training's taken years
It wasn't the winning alone that was worth the work and the tears.
The applause will be forgotten, the prize will be misplaced
But the long hard hours of practice will never be a waste.
For in trying to win you build a skill
You learn that winning depends on will.
You never grow by how much you win
You only grow by how much you put in.
So any new challenge you've just begun
Put forth your best...and you've already won.   - W.A. Clennan

Action items for making it a positive week.
1. Make a list of things that give you hope.
2. Make a special effort to gaze at the moon one night. Take a few
    deep breaths and relax.
3. Try to put some love in all your chores today. Even the
    mundane deserves your best effort.
4. Make a promise to someone that you can keep and fulfill.

5. Show your appreciation to your employees and co-workers with a card, a batch of homemade cookies or a box of donuts.

One of the major keys of success is Persistence. The stonecutter hammers away at the rock, perhaps a hundred times without as much as a crack showing in it. Yet at the one hundred-and-first blow it will split in two, and you know it was not the last blow that did it, but all that had gone before.

The object of education is to prepare the young to educate themselves throughout their lives. - Robert Maynard Hutchins

To learn something new, take the path you took yesterday.
- John Burroughs

In the month of May comes thoughts of graduation and the passage from one stage of life to another. The following is good advice for any of us going from one stage to another.
Children's books author Theodor Seuss Geisel - better know as Dr. Seuss - gave the following address at Lake Forest College in Illinois. "It seems to be behooven upon me to bring forth great words of wisdom to this graduating class as it leaves these cloistered halls to enter the outside world. Fortunately, my wisdom is in very short supply, and I have managed to condense everything I know into this epic poem consisting of 14 lines:
My Uncle Terwilliger on the Art of Eating Popovers
My uncle ordered popovers
from the restaurant's bill of fare.
And, when they were served, he regarded them
with a penetrating stare. . .
Then he spoke great Words of Wisdom

as he sat there on that chair:
"To eat these things," said my uncle,
"You must exercise great care.
You may swallow down what's solid...
BUT...you must spit out the air!"
And...as you partake of the world's bill of fare,
that's darned good advice to follow.
Do a lot of spitting out the hot air.
And be careful what you swallow.

Many years ago a man picked up the morning newspaper and, to his horror, read his own obituary. The newspaper had reported the death of the wrong man. Like most of us, he relished the idea of finding out what people would say about him after he died. He read past the bold caption which read, "Dynamite King dies," to the text itself. He read along until he was taken aback by the description of him as a "merchant of death."
He was the inventor of dynamite and had amassed a great fortune from the manufacture of weapons of destruction. But he was moved by this description. Did he really want to be known as a "merchant of death"?
It was at that moment that a healing power greater than the destructive force of dynamite came over him. It was his hour of conversion. From that point on, he devoted his energy and money to works of peace and human betterment. Today, of course, he is best remembered, not as a "merchant of death," but as the founder of the Nobel Peace Prize - Alfred Nobel.

Start the month off right.
1. Surprise someone with a heartfelt gesture of friendship.
2. Make a point to spread as much good news as you can - all day.

3. Pass up a parking spot. Park a little further away and enjoy the extra exercise.
4. As a family, do something to help someone else.
5. Schedule a "be kind to" day for every family member, co-worker, employee or friend. Try to surprise each honoree.

No matter how bad things may look to you - Remember - there are other people who think your side looks greener.

A good name, like good will, is got by many actions and lost by one. - Lord Jeffery

Only those who risk going too far can possibly find out how far one can go. - T.S. Eliot

The following are the Positive Powered Winners! A-B-C's of Achievement.
Affirm the positives about yourself. I feel fantastic, great, super, terrific and wonderful.
Believe that you can achieve your dreams.
Champion the good causes that help other people achieve.
Doers are people who do whatever it takes to be successful.
Enthusiastic people make things happen.
Fantastic is how positive people feel.
Goals help you achieve success.
Humor helps you to relieve the stress in your live.
Imagineering is the way to plan your future.
Joy is yours through accomplishment.
Knowledge is a key to achievement.
Laughter keeps you healthy.
Motivation comes from within your positive self.

Positive People Power

Never give up, never give up, never give up.
One person controls your thoughts - y o u!
Personal positive power leads to productivity.
Quest after your hopes, dreams and ambitions.
Reward yourself with each goal victory.
Smile is the best make-up you can wear.
Terrific is the feeling of champions.
Understand that you are willing to pay the price.
Visualize your dreams coming true.
Winners say "YES" to adventure.
Xcellent is the grade worth aiming for.
You are the best and the greatest.
Zest in everything you do.

Sir Edmund Hillary was the first man to climb Mount Everest. On May 29, 1953, he scaled the highest mountain then know to man - 29,000 feet. He was knighted for his efforts. What was the motivation for Hillary wanting to be the man to make this achievement. Well, in 1952 he attempted to climb Mount Everest and failed. A few weeks later a group in England asked him to speak to its members. Hillary walked on stage to a thunderous applause. The audience was recognizing an attempt at greatness, but Edmund Hillary saw himself as a failure. He walked to the edge of the stage, made a fist and pointed at a picture of the mountain. He said in a loud voice, "Mount Everest, you beat me the first time, but I'll beat you the next time because you've grown all you are going to grow **...but I'm still growing!"**

Ideas for Winners for the coming week:
1. Share a dream with someone who may be able to help you attain it.

41

2. Give yourself more time by choosing to let go of something that really isn't all that important.
3. Find a half-hour to just sit and be still. Listen to what is in your heart. Then act upon it.
4. When you put out the trash this week, tape a thank-you note to the top of it.
5. Whistle while you work - even if it is only in your mind.

Do you spend all your time earning a living and never stop to live your earnings?

If you're not using your smile, you're like a man with a million dollars in the bank and no checkbook. - Les Giblin

Persistence is...continuing to work toward the achievement of a goal or the completion of a task despite seemingly insurmountable obstacles.

Are you an average American? If so, Thank You!!!
Most of you are the kind of people that make America great.
No, most of you won't appear on any "most admired list."
But, each of you represent the average American, the hard-working men and women who are the backbone of our country. The average folks who love their families, are good neighbors, respect the law, work hard at their jobs, pay their bills and pay their taxes. Not the headline-grabbers, just ordinary people, often overlooked and usually taken for granted.

And what of our average Americans? They could feel penalized for working hard and just say, "What's the use?" Instead, they are faithful to their jobs, even if bored at times. They work hard, not to please an employer, but to satisfy their integrity. They start out to do something and they accomplish it. They have compassion for their neighbor's failings, but won't allow their values to be compromised to make him look good. They help the weak by setting an example of strength.

God bless you, the average American. You might have enjoyed an extra hour of sleep, but you didn't; you might want to quit, but won't. You are what makes America great.

There are no great people in this world, there are only ordinary people. The only difference is that some people set higher goals, dream bigger dreams, and settle for nothing less than the best. The truth is, the person who set low goals achieves little. The size of the dream will determine the size of the person you will become.
Excellence is the motto of great people. All-out effort is the hallmark of their character. Remember, if you aim at nothing - you're sure to hit it.
The human being is the only creature in the universe that has the divine quality of dreaming.
What you want to be
Where you want to go
What you'd love to do
Goals you'd like to reach
The greatest power in the world is a positive idea.
Wouldn't you rather attempt to do something great and fail, than attempt to do nothing and succeed.
Action Items for this week:
1. Be goofy today. Do silly things that bring you joy, either alone or with a prized friend.
2. As the phone company says, reach out and touch someone, with a phone call or letter.

3. Spend some time in nature. Listen to the sounds and admire the beauty around you.
4. Are you celebrating the long weekend? Don't forget why you've got it.
5. Display your flag to honor those who gave us the freedom to live in America.

The more faith you have, the more you believe,
The more goals you set, the more you'll achieve.
So reach for the stars, pick a mountain to climb,
Dare to think big, but give yourself time.
Remember no matter how futile things seem,
With faith, there is no Impossible Dream!

Strange how much you've got to know before you know how little you know. - Duncan Stuart

True success is overcoming the fear of being unsuccessful. - Paul Sweeney

It is not half as important to burn the midnight oil as it is to be awake in the daytime. - E.W. Elmore

The following keys can be used in the coming week to add happiness and joy to your life and to others.
TWENTY KEYS TO A HAPPY LIFE
1. Compliment three people everyday.
2. Watch a sunrise.
3. Be the first to say "Hello."
4. Live beneath your means.

5. Treat everyone as you want to be treated.
6. Never give up on anybody, miracles happen.
7. Forget the Joneses.
8. Remember someone's name.
9. Pray not for things, but for wisdom and courage.
10. Be tough-minded, but tender hearted.
11. Be kinder than you have to be.
12. Don't forget that a person's greatest emotional need is to feel appreciated.
13. Keep your promises.
14. Learn to show cheerfulness even when you don't feel it.
15. Remember that overnight success usually takes 15 years.
16. Leave everything better than you found it.
17. Remember that winners do what losers don't want to do.
18. When you arrive at your job in the morning, let the first thing you say brighten everyone's day.
19. Don't rain on other people's parades.
20. Don't waste an opportunity to tell someone you love them.

God gave each of us a bag of tools,
A shapeless mass and a book of rules.
What we make is each our own,
A stumbling block or a stepping stone.

If the cost of education continues to rise, education will become as expensive as ignorance. - Travelers Mutual Insurance

The opportunities of man are limited only by his imagination. But so few have imagination that there are ten thousand fiddlers to one composer. - Charles Kettering

Positive People Power

So much of what we intend to do is going to be done tomorrow. In a sense it can be said that tomorrow will be the most wonderful day in history, for that is the day when most of us are going to begin to do better. But today is the "tomorrow" that you looked at yesterday. You could begin today to do better and be better. Why put it off? You'll never find a better day than today to begin to be what you've always wanted to be, to begin to live your dream instead of just dreaming it. Don't allow your desires to become museum pieces!
- Sunshine

What is the one thing you want in life more than anything else? Regardless of what you would like to be, have, or do, you must stimulate within your mind an intense desire for its attainment. You must know exactly what it is you want from life and then transform this wish into an obsession that is unstoppable; one that know no defeat. Going after your dreams only halfheartedly will if anything, produce only minimal results. When you develop within yourself an intense burning desire and you want something bad enough, nothing will be able to persuade you that it's not possible. Where there is a will, there is always a way. Desire is another word for focused energy. It becomes the inward motivating force that propels us toward achievement in all endeavors.

An old farmer had plowed around a large rock in one of his fields for years. He had broken several plowshares and a cultivator on it and had grown rather morbid about the rock.
After breaking another plowshare one day, and remembering all the trouble the rock had caused him through the years, he finally decided to do something about it.
When he put the crowbar under the rock, he was surprised to discover that it was only about six inches thick and that he could break it up

46

easily with a sledgehammer. As he was carting the pieces away he had to smile, remembering all the trouble that the rock had caused him over the years and how easy it would have been to get rid of it sooner.

Are there rocks in your life that are causing you trouble, but that probably can be removed very easily? Look carefully at the roadblocks in your life and make an effort to do something creative and constructive about them. Don't let them drain energy from the goals you have set for your success.

TO DO list for the coming week:
1. Make a point to give thanks for the blessings you receive each day.
2. Write an encouraging letter to someone who has provided you with good service.
3. Share an overheard compliment and forget an overheard criticism.
4. Find a need and fill it.
5. Shine your light of enthusiasm on someone who needs a little light in their lives.

If you want the rainbows, you gotta put up with the rain.
- Dolly Parton

If opportunity doesn't knock, build a door. - Milton Berle

Success isn't how far you got, but the distance you traveled from where you started.

Eagles don't flock. You have to find them one at a time.
- Ross Perot

THE WINNER:
* Controls his own destiny.
* Has specific goals and plans for achieving them.
* Reviews his activities and priorities.
* Solves problems, makes decisions and takes action.
* Manages his time effectively.
* Focuses his energy on high-payoff activities.
* Completes tasks according to priorities.
* Seeks and enjoys new experiences.
* Invests free time in self-improvement.
* Is open to new ideas from reading and attending courses.
* Balances hard work with rest and relaxation.
* Reviews goals and makes changes when needed.
* Acts friendly and affirmatively towards others.
* Serves the needs of others.
* Negotiates for what he wants.
* Asserts his own rights, interests and values.
* Takes events in stride, accepts and adapts to setbacks.
* Maintains a positive attitude.
* Laughs easily and has a good sense of humor.
* Maintains a high sense of self-esteem.

60% of the people do not set goals.
10% of the people set goals, but do not write them down.
3% of the people set goals and write them down.
The 3% group do 50 times more than all the others put together.
They are WINNERS!

Set your goals high - go after them with burning determination - let nothing stop you. Your greatest satisfaction will be the exhilaration of achievement. Your dreams are within reach. This fast changing world cries out for new ideas and the people who work to transform ideas into reality will be handsomely rewarded. You have within you, all the power you need to achieve whatever you desire. No matter what "believe you can do it and you will!"

An old mountaineer from West Virginia was celebrated for his wisdom. "Uncle Zed," a young man asked, "how did you get so wise?"
"Weren't hard," said the old man. "I've got good judgment. Good judgment comes from experience. And experience - well, that comes from having bad judgment."

Whoever said "It's not whether you win or lose that counts" probably lost. - Martina Navratilova

A nation without heroes is a nation without a future. - Mary Mannes

Love is an act of faith, and whoever is of little faith is also of little love. - Erich Fromm

A smile is a light on your face that lets people know that your heart is at home!

The only true gift is a portion of thyself. You don't have to spend money to give something of value, Give of yourself and give a smile!

A smile costs nothing, but gives much. It enriches those who receive, without making poorer those who give. It takes but a moment, but the memory of it sometimes lasts forever. None is so rich or mighty that he can get along without it, and none is so poor but that he can be made rich by it. A smile creates happiness in the home, fosters good will in business, and is the countersign of friendship. It brings rest to the weary, cheer to the discouraged, sunshine to the sad, and it is nature's best antidote for trouble. Yet it cannot be bought, begged, borrowed, or stolen, for it is something that is of no value to anyone until it is given away. Some people are too tired to give you a smile. Give then one of yours, as none needs a smile so much as he who has no more to give.

To make a further impact with your smile, add a kind word, a touch on the arm, a pat on the back, a hug or any proper touching to add emphasis to your remarks. Any kind of touching gesture combined with a compliment will make the other person feel better and you will feel better also. Just pass on a nice, warm smile and a kind or generous word, like "Hi, I feel great and I hope you do, too!" This sharing is a win-win situation at its best. Now two people feel good about themselves and about each other. It has been said that the following are the sweetest phrases in the English language that people like to hear. The phrases are:

"I love you"

"Let's go out to dinner"

"All is forgiven"

"You can sleep until noon"

"Keep the change"

"You've lost weight"

"Thank You"

To Do List for the Coming Week:

1. Is there an overdue thank-you note you've been meaning to send? Do it today.
2. Share your day with loved ones. What can you do to make it special?

3. Get up fifteen minutes earlier and spend the time in quiet reflection. How does it affect your day?
4. Coax a smile out of two sour faces. Tell a joke, give a hug, or leave a funny card.
5. Do something nice for your body. Eat healthier, exercise a bit longer, or take a hot bath.

A man was bothered with continual ringing in his ears, bulging eyes, and a flushed face. Over a period of three years he went to one doctor after another. One took out his tonsils, one removed his appendix, another pulled out all his teeth. He even tried a goat-gland treatment in Switzerland - all to no avail. Finally, one doctor told him there was no hope - he had six months to live.
The poor fellow quit his job, sold all his belongings and decided to live it up in the time he had left. He went to his tailor and ordered several suits and shirts. The tailor measured his neck and wrote down "16 1/2'
The man corrected him. "It's 15 1/2", he said.
The tailor measured again: "16 1/2."
But the man insisted that he'd always worn a size 15 1/2.
"Well, all right," said the tailor. "Just don't come back here complaining if you have ringing ears, bulging eyes and a flushed face."

The following would be appropriate for the 4th of July celebration or any day, to help us remember what a great country America is.

THE PLEDGE OF ALLEGIANCE

From THE RED SKELTON HOUR, January 14, 1969

Positive People Power

On January 14, 1969, Red Skelton presented "The Little Old Man" as a teacher. The time was 1923. The students had finished reciting the Pledge of Allegiance which at that time was but 10 years old. The old sage called the children together and said --

"Boys and girls, I have been listening to you recite the Pledge of Allegiance all semester and it appears that it has become monotonous to you or could it be you do not know the meaning of those words. If I may, I would like to recite the Pledge and give to you a definition of the words.

I - meaning me, an individual, a committee of one.
Pledge - dedicate all of my worldly goods to give without self-pity.

Allegiance - my love and devotion.

To the Flag - our standard, Old Glory, a symbol of freedom. Wherever she waves, there is respect because your loyalty has given her a dignity that shouts freedom is everybody's job.

Of the United - that means that we have all come together.

States Of America.- individual communities that have united into 48 great states. 48 individual communities with pride and dignity and purpose, all divided with imaginary boundaries, yet united to a common cause, and that's love of country.

And to the Republic - a republic, a state in which sovereign power is invested in representatives chosen by the people to govern. And government is the people and it's from the people to the leaders, not from the leaders to the people.

 **For which it stands!**

One nation - meaning, so blessed by God.

Indivisible - incapable of being divided.

With Liberty - which is freedom and the right of power to live one's life without threats or fear or any sort of retaliation.

And justice - The principle and quality of dealing fairly with others.

For all - which means, boys and girls, it's as much your country as it is mine."

Since I was a small boy, two states have been added to our nation, and two words have been added to the Pledge of Allegiance - "under God."

Wouldn't it be a pity if someone said, "That's a prayer" and that would be eliminated from schools, too?

PLEDGE TO THE FLAG is a solemn promise of allegiance to the United States. It reads:

**I pledge allegiance to the flag of the United States of America
and to the Republic for which it stands,
one Nation under God,
Indivisible,
with liberty and justice for all.**

Public-school children first recited the pledge as they saluted the flag during the National School Celebration held in 1892. President Benjamin Harrison had called for patriotic exercises in schools to mark the 400th anniversary of the discovery of America. Francis Bellamy of Boston, an associate editor of The Youth's Companion, wrote the original pledge. The National Flag Conferences of the American Legion expanded the original wording in 1923 and 1924. In 1942, Congress made the pledge part of its code for the use of the flag. In 1954, it added the words "under God."

Will Rogers said it: "Instead of giving money to found colleges to promote learning, why don't they pass a constitutional amendment, prohibiting anybody from learning anything. And if it works as good as the prohibition once did, why, in five years we would have the smartest race of people on earth."

There's an old legend about a tribe that was always at war with other tribes. They murdered, raped and pillaged. They had no morals, love, or compassion. They were so violent, they seemed to have a death wish.
An alarmed elder called together some reasonable members from all the other tribes to try and save the violent tribe's people from themselves. After much discussion the reasonable people decided to take the secret of success and happiness away from those who abused it and hide it from them.

But where should this secret be hidden? Some suggested it be buried deep in the earth. Others said to put it on the highest mountain. Still others suggested it be sunk deep in the ocean. There was no agreement until the elder who had gathered them together made this proposal. "Let us hide the secret within the people themselves," he suggested. "People like this will never find happiness and success there."

To this day people have been feverishly pursuing success and happiness, searching for the secret. Relatively few ever find its hiding place -- already within themselves. It is there, but only you can bring it from its hiding place and use it for abundant good. Let your integrity be the building force for your success.

Whether you know it or not, you are on a journey. You had no choice about when or where it started. You don't know when, where or how it will end. All you know for sure is that it's bound to end sometime. There are rules that apply to this journey, but you've had to learn them as you go. And for the most part, you cannot control them. You may not know the purpose of your journey, even though others claim to know.

All you know is that once started, you must continue every day, whether you feel like it or not. You start with no possessions, and when you finish you must turn in all you have accumulated. In the end, some say you will be rewarded or punished. But how do they know for sure?

That's life, and you cannot change it. A little faith and a sense of humor, fortunately, help to cushion some of the bumps. And the bumps - both good and bad - are what life is all about. Live life as if each day is your last, because one day it will be, and we are not given the time of our departure. Live your life positively and the results will be positively amazing.

Positive People Power

Your To Do List for the coming week:
1. Make a list of your five favorite positive words and stick it where you will see it at least five times a day.
2. Count your blessings. Number them and write them down. Can you top 100?
3. Summer is here! Have a pool party or get the hose out and play water games.
4. Enjoy the long days. Take an evening walk and relax after the sunset.
5. Do some volunteer work today - at your church, in your neighborhood or in your community.

Plan ahead - it wasn't raining when Noah built the Ark.

Abraham Lincoln said it: Determine that the thing can and shall be done, and then we shall find the way.
In other words, before the way in which a thing can be done can be understood, two things must happen and they must happen in us. One, we must be convinced that the thing can be done. It isn't enough simply to wish it could be done, or merely hope that we can be successful in it. We must <u>know</u> it can be done - and by us.
Two, we must be determined that it will be done and by us. We must have made the decision to do it.
Don't we all have a collection of varied plans that we're going to do "someday"? But we haven't really made a decision on which one we're going to put into action first. They're not our plans for today. And they're not on tomorrow's schedule either. They're on the schedule for "someday" and "someday" usually turns out to be no day.

These great ideas of ours aren't really plans at all. They're still in the dream stage. They're just wishes and as Washington Irving once said, "Little minds have wishes, great minds have purposes."

It's fine to build castles in the air - provided we don't become too satisfied with just leaving them there.

There is one necessary step if we are to use our castles in the air as patterns, and then really get them built: we must make plans to move into those castles.

Determine that you can and that you will, and you will find the way. Now, follow through on that decision. From all your unfilled plans - your castles in the air - choose one as your first objective. Now, select one definite step - one definite thing you can do toward that objective. Next, put that one step definitely on your schedule to be started at a specific time. Perhaps it will be this morning at nine o'clock or this evening at six o'clock. You name it and when the time comes, let nothing stand in the way of your starting it.

Do this and you'll have one of the most satisfying feelings inside you that you've had in years.

Experience is not what happens to a man. It is what a man does with what happens to him. - Aldous Huxley

I do not believe in a fate that falls on men however they act, but I do believe in a fate that falls on them unless they act. - G.K. Chesterton

Discipline is inevitable; if it does not come from within a man, it will be imposed from without. - David Grayson

A young freelance artist tried to sell his sketches to a number of newspapers. They all turned him down. One Kansas City editor told him he had no talent.

But he had faith in his ability and kept trying to sell his work. Finally he got a job making drawings for church publicity material. He rented a mouse-infested garage to turn out his sketches, and he continued to produce free-lance drawings in hopes that someone would buy them.

One of the mice in the garage must have inspired him, for he created a cartoon character called Mickey Mouse. Walt Disney was on his way.

Enjoy yourself. These are the good old days you're going to miss in the years ahead.

Experience is knowing a lot of things you shouldn't do. - Bill Knudsen

<u>Tip:</u> In regards to name tags. Always wear your name tags on your right side. This puts your name in the line of sight as someone approaches and extends their hand. They can look directly at your name and if their name tag is on the right hand side, you can look directly at theirs. If avoids the awkward move of both of you leaning your head over to view the name.

A technique for finding out more information is to repeat the last statement made as a question. Example: Well, I found that the price was out of line.

"Out of Line?" Yes, in comparison to some of the other stores.

"Some of the other stores?" Yes, I went to A&P and Food Lion and their prices seemed to be more in line with what I wanted to pay.

"What you wanted to pay?" I thought the $10 - $20 range for that type of product was more than fair considering the labor costs.

"The labor cost?"............well, you can see how this would work. But be advised not to use it too long or the other person will tire of answering your questions and think you don't understand at all.

You make a living by what you get, but you make a life by what you give.

Do you tend to be impulsive? If so, and if your job involves handling people, better slow down. Don't make decisions hastily that involve other people. Take your time and look the situation over from all angles first.

Chances are, when you act impulsively you've only considered one point of view - your own. Take time to think of how this situation will look to the other people involved.

Two good ways to cut down on impulsive decisions are (1) try to anticipate situations that will arise and think about them in advance, (2) don't hurry decisions unnecessarily. Put your first impulse away for a few hours or a day before you act on it. Then take another look at all sides of the question before you do.

Before you contact other people - even on matters that may seem fairly routine to you - put yourself in their shoes, and think over what their point of view is likely to be. How will it look to them? How will it affect their pride, their job status, their satisfaction? If you were they, what would you object to?

By sympathizing with other people's points of view, you make finding a satisfactory middle ground a lot easier.

The solutions to problems are not necessarily found in new and brilliant ideas. They are sometimes discovered by making the old, proven ideas work, such as an honest day's work, respect for the given word, living within income, and the willingness to make necessary sacrifices to attain a worthwhile goal.

Pros are people who do their jobs well even when they don't feel like it.

Motivational
Moments

"I keep the telephone of my mind open to
peace, harmony, health, love and
abundance.
Then whenever doubt, anxiety, or fear try
to
call me, they keep getting a busy signal
and soon they'll forget my number."
Edith Armstrong

61

Positive People Power

Go as far as you can see; when you get there, you will be able to see further. - Thomas Carlyle

Be yourself. Who else is better qualified? - Frank Giblin

With three brushes in each hand, Denny Dent paints portraits on six-foot canvasses in the time it take to play a few carefully selected pieces of music. Whether painting Jack Nicklaus, General Colin Powell or Martin Luther King, Jr., the power and integrity is always the same. The artist himself refers to his work as "a passionate dance on canvas," and those who have seen his creations are compelled to agree. Denny has been described as the world's only "rock and roll painter." This title refers to his original repertoire which featured Denny's renderings of music's greatest acts including: Beethoven, Frank Sinatra, Elton John, Garth Brooks, John Lennon, Tina Turner and Billy Joel to name a few.
His message is simple: "It's not what you do, it's the way you do it that makes you an artist. Whatever you do...do it with all your heart. Be what you are...be creative! "

Can't is the worst word that's written or spoken,
Doing more harm than slander and lies,
On it is many a strong spirit broken,
And with it many a good purpose dies.
It springs from the lips of the thoughtless each morning,
And robs us of courage we need through the day.
It rings in our ears like a timely-sent warning,
And laughs when we falter and fall by the way.

I was standing in line at the grocery store recently and the lady in front of me was wearing a T-shirt that had the following words:
Let those who love us, love us.
As for those that don't love us,
Let God turn their hearts.
And if He can't turn their hearts,
May He turn their ankles,
So we may know them by their limp.

There's a story about the California Gold Rush that tells of two brothers who sold all they had and went prospecting for gold. They discovered a vein of the shining ore, staked a claim, and proceeded to get down to the serious business of getting the gold out of the mine. All went well at first, but then a strange thing happened. The vein of gold ore disappeared. They had come to the end of the rainbow and the pot of gold was no longer there. The brothers continued to pick away, but without success. Finally, they gave up in disgust.
They sold their equipment and claim rights for a few hundred dollars, and took the train back home. Now the man who bought the claim hired an engineer to examine the rock strata of the mind. The engineer advised him to continue digging in the same spot where the former owners had left off. And three feet deeper, the new owner struck gold. A little more persistence and the two brothers would have been millionaires themselves.
There's gold in you too!
Do you need to dig three feet farther?

Children are not things to be molded, but are people to be unfolded.
- Jess Lair

Youth is when you blame all your troubles on your parents; maturity is when you learn that everything is the fault of the younger generation. - Harold Coffin

With summer ending and school starting, I thought these memos would be helpful to those of you with children or grandchildren. However, these memos can also be appropriate in some situations between employer/employee, teacher/student, husband/wife or any relationship where two or more are gathered.

TWENTY MEMOS FROM A CHILD

1. Don't spoil me. I know quite well I ought not to have all I ask for. I am only testing you.
2. Don't be afraid to be firm with me. I prefer it; it makes me feel more secure.
3. Don't let me form bad habits. I have to rely on you to detect them in the early stages.
4. Don't make me feel smaller than I am. It only makes me behave stupidly "big."
5. Don't correct me in front of people if you can help it. I'll take much more notice if you talk quietly in private.
6. Don't protect me from consequences. I need to learn the painful way sometimes.
7. Don't make me feel my mistakes are sins.
8. Don't be too upset when I say "I hate you." It isn't you I hate, but your power to thwart me.
9. Don't nag. If you do, I shall have to protect myself by appearing deaf.
10. Don't tax my honesty too much. I'm easily frightened into telling lies.

11. Don't make rash promises. Remember that I feel badly let down when promises are broken.
12. Don't forget that I cannot explain myself as well as I should like. This is why I am not always very accurate.
13. Don't be inconsistent. It completely confuses me and makes me lose my faith in you.
14. Don't push (put) me off when I ask questions. If you do, you will find that I stop asking and seek my information elsewhere.
15. Don't tell me my fears are silly. They are very real and you can do much to reassure me, if you try to understand.
16. Don't ever think it is beneath your dignity to apologize to me. An honest apology makes me surprisingly warm towards you.
17. Don't ever suggest that you are perfect or infallible. It gives me too great a shock when I discover that you are neither.
18. Don't forget I love experimenting. I couldn't get on without it, so please put up with it.
19. Don't forget how quickly I am growing up. It must be very difficult for you to keep pace with me, but please try.
20. Don't forget that I can't thrive without lots of understanding and love.

You cannot do a kindness too soon, for you never know how soon it will be too late. - Ralph Waldo Emerson

It's the man who waits for his ship to come in who's always missing the boat.

An economist was asked to talk to a group of business people about the recession. She tacked up a big sheet of white paper. Then she made a black spot on the paper with her pencil and asked a man in the front row what he saw. The man replied promptly, "A black spot."

Positive People Power

The speaker asked every person the same question, and each replied, "A black spot."
With calm and deliberate emphasis the speaker said: "Yes, there is a little black spot, but none of you mentioned the big sheet of white paper. And that is my speech."
What are you seeing in your life? Are you seeing only the negative and making mountains out of molehills? Or are you seeing the positives and making your goals, plans and dreams come true? Make sure you are a Positive Winner and seek to find the treasures that lie within your reach!

Why can't life's big problems come when we are twenty and know everything.

Thank God that every morning when you get up that you have something to do which must be done, whether you like it or not. Being forced to work, and forced to do your best, will breed in you a hundred virtues which the idle will never know. - Charles Kingsley

When you try to make an impression, the chances are that is the impression you will make.

When Americans make sandwiches, they use square bread, round meats, rectangular pickles, slices of tomatoes, chopped onions, flat lettuce, and two kinds of slippery spread. They then cut the sandwich diagonally and complain when everything falls out of it.

On a clear, bright sunny day take a powerful magnifying glass and a stack of newspapers and go outside for an experiment. Hold the magnifying glass over a pile of crumpled pages. Even though you are magnifying the power of the sun's rays through the glass lens, you will never start a fire - if you keep moving the glass.

But if you hold the magnifying glass still, allowing it to focus the rays in a concentrated beam of sun energy, you harness the power of the sun and multiply it through the lens - starting a fire.

Focusing also works with your power of thought! Try it and ignite your wandering ideas.

Positive activities for the coming week:
1. Attempt something great.
2. Make a commitment.
3. Share these writings.
4. Keep your word.
5. Be humble.
6. Avoid put-downs.

The greatest ability is dependability. - Curt Bergwall

We expect perfection from our heroes and kids - but settle for so much less from ourselves.

A pro is always at his best - Regardless!

Happiness is the experience of having lived a life that you feel is worthwhile. Happiness is the natural experience of winning your own self-respect, as well as the respect of others. You can't smoke, inhale, or snort happiness. You can't buy it, drive it, fly it, swallow it, inject it or travel to it. Happiness is the journey, not the destination. Happiness comes only to those who feel it without chasing it and who can give it away without expecting a payoff.

Positive People Power

We can count the day as lost is we haven't said something good or complimented someone.

Several years ago a newspaper in Nashville, Tennessee, ran a feature story about a dairy farmer. Complete and thorough records had been maintained regarding each cow's production.

The reporter told about one cow that had been sold for hamburger after she had kicked the farmer the second time. He questioned the farmer about the practicality of selling a valuable animal which could produce so much milk.

The farmer's reply was a classic. "Life's too short to spend it with a kicking cow."

Fear, anxiety, and worry all contribute to various psychosomatic ailments. Why should we let fear of criticism, anxiety connected with a frustrating job, and worry about things that will probably never happen give us ulcers, high blood pressure, and dozens of ailments? Life is too short to spend it with a kicking cow.

After years of study and experimentation psychologists now seem to have arrived at this very important truth: The pleasure of reward motivates people more than the pain of punishment. And the statement holds true whether we are dealing with a worker in a factory, a child in a home, or a lion in the jungle.

It means that people will be motivated to work more by the expectations of pleasure (the satisfactions derived from work) that by fear of losing their jobs.

It means that children will be motivated toward good conduct more by the pleasure of receiving love from their parents that they will from fear of being punished.

It means that you train the savage beast not with a whip but a morsel!

See how you can work this philosophy into your daily activities and you will be amazed at the results.

A hungry mountain lion came out of the hills to stalk a grazing herd. The lion attacked a bull and killed it. As it feasted on its kill, the lion paused from time to time to let out a scream in triumph.

A hunter, who was in the area, heard the commotion, found the mountain lion and shot it dead.

The moral of the story: When you're full of bull, keep your mouth shut.

The journey in between what you once were and who you are now becoming is where the dance of life really takes place.
- Barbara DeAngelis

You were born with wings. Why prefer to crawl through life? - Rumi

-From *The Velveteen Rabbit* by Margery Williams

The Skin Horse had lived longer in the nursery than any of the others. He was so old that his brown coat was bald in patches and showed the seams underneath, and most of the hairs in his tail had been pulled out to string bead necklaces. He was wise, for he had seen a long succession of mechanical toys arrive to boast and swagger, and by-and-by break their mainsprings and pass away, and he knew that they were only toys, and would never turn into anything else. For nursery magic is very strange and wonderful, and only those playthings that are old and wise and experienced like the Skin Horse understand all about it.

"What is REAL?" asked the [Velveteen] Rabbit one day, when they were lying side by side near the nursery fender, before

69

Nana came to tidy the room. "Does it mean having things that buzz inside you and a stick-out handle?"

"Real isn't how you are made," said the Skin Horse. "It's a thing that happens to you. When a child loves you for a long, long time, not just to play with, but REALLY loves you, then you become Real."

"Does it hurt?" asked the Rabbit.

"Sometimes," said the Skin Horse, for he was always truthful. "When you are Real you don't mind being hurt."

"Does it happen all at once, like being wound up," he asked, "or bit by bit?"

"It doesn't happen all at once," said the Skin Horse. "You become. It takes a long time. That's why it doesn't often happen to people who break easily, or have sharp edges, or who have to be carefully kept. Generally, by the time you are Real, most of your hair has been loved off, and your eyes drop out and you get loose in the joints and very shabby. But these things don't matter at all, because once you are Real you can't be ugly, except to people who don't understand."

*Are you real to the people around you. Do you really love others and have you shown your love for a long, long time - because then you become Real.

- From Dr. Seuss - Oh, the Places You'll Go!
You have brains in your head, you have feet in your shoes,
You can steer yourself any direction you choose.
You're on your own, and you know what you know.
And you are the person who'll decide where to go.

Here are some activities to make this week positive for you and those around you.

Positive People Power

Superb Sunday - Attend the church of your choice
Marvelous Monday - Speak only kind words
Terrific Tuesday - Have dinner with family or friends
Wonderful Wednesday - Listen to your heart
Tremendous Thursday - Smile at least 25 times
Fantastic Friday - Stretch yourself mentally
Super Saturday - Try, try again

Begin the day with friendliness, and only friends you'll find.
Yes, greet the dawn with happiness; keep happy thoughts in mind.
Salute the day with peaceful thoughts, and peace will fill your heart;
Begin the day with joyful soul, and joy will be your part.
Begin the day with friendliness. Keep friendly all day long.
Keep in your soul a friendly thought, your heart a friendly song.
Have in your mind a word of cheer for all who come your way.
And they will bless you, too, in turn, and wish you "Happy day."
Begin each day with friendly thoughts, and as the day goes on,
Stay friendly, loving, good and kind, just as you were at dawn.
The day will be a friendly one, and then at night you'll find
That you were happy all day long- through friendly thoughts in mind.
- Frank B. Whitney

Only he who attempts the ridiculous can achieve the impossible.
 - Will Henry

Barbra Streisand sang about People who need People are the luckiest
people in the world. Well, the whole world needs people.
People - who cannot be bought.
Whose word is their bond.
Who put character above wealth.
Who possess opinions and a will.

71

Who do not hesitate to take chances.
Who will make no compromise with wrong.
Who will not lose their individuality in a crowd.
Who will be as honest in small things as in great things.
Who will not say they do it "because everybody else does it."
Whose ambitions are not confined to their own selfish desires.
Who will not have one brand of honesty for business purposes and another for private life.
Who are true to their friends in adversity as well as prosperity.
Who do not believe that shrewdness, sharpness, and cunning are the best qualities for winning success.
Who are not ashamed or afraid to stand for the truth when it is unpopular, who can say "yes" with emphasis, although the rest of the world says "no."

In the "Star War" movie, *The Empire Strikes Back*, Luke Skywalker flies his X-wing ship to a swamp planet on a personal quest. There he seeks out a Jedi master named Yoda to teach him the ways of becoming a Jedi warrior. Luke wants to free the galaxy from the oppression of the evil tyrant, Darth Vader.
Yoda reluctantly agrees to help Luke and begins by teaching him how to lift rocks with his mental powers.
Then, one day, Yoda tell Luke to lift his ship out from the swamp where it sank after a crash landing. Luke complains that lifting rocks is one thing, but lifting a star-fighter is quite another matter. Yoda insists. Luke manages a valiant effort but fails in his attempt.
Yoda then focuses his mind, and lifts out the ship with ease. Luke, dismayed, exclaims, "I don't believe it.!"
"That's why you couldn't lift it," Yoda replied, "You didn't believe you could."

THE POWER OF ONE

He was born in an obscure village.
He was the child of a peasant woman.
He grew up in another obscure village.
He worked in a carpenter shop until He was thirty.
He then became an itinerant preacher.
He never wrote a book.
He never had a family of His own.
He never went to a theater.
He never visited a big city.
He never traveled over two hundred miles from His birthplace.
His preaching aroused the authorities who arrested Him.
His friends deserted Him.
His closest friend denied he even knew Him.
He suffered the mockery of being nailed upon a cross.
His executioners gambled for His only property...His robe.
He was placed in a borrowed grave through the pity of a friend.
He would never be heard from again, they predicted...
and then there was Easter Sunday!
Nineteen centuries have come and gone, and today He is the central figure of the human race. All the armies that ever marched, all the navies that ever sailed, all the parliaments that ever sat, and all the kings that ever reigned have not affected the life of man on this earth as much as that One Solitary Life.

BY JUST ONE VOTE...

"Why should I bother to vote? One vote doesn't make any difference, anyhow!" That old familiar refrain. But before you sell yourself on the concept, take a look at history.

By *just one vote*, Rutherford B. Hayes was elected President in 1878. His election was contested and referred to an electoral commission. That *just one vote* was cast by a voter who, though desperately ill, insisted on being taken to the polls.

By *just one vote*, Thomas Jefferson was elected President in 1800 by the Electoral College.

By *just one vote*, Adoph Hitler was elected Chancellor of Germany.

By *just one vote*, President Andrew Johnson was saved from impeachment.

By *just one vote*, Texas, Washington, California, Idaho and Oregon gained statehood.

AND By *just one vote*, the Continental Congress decided that *English* would be the official language of the United States instead of *German*.

So always VOTE!!! Because your one vote is important.

ONE IS A BIG NUMBER

One song can spark a moment, One flower can wake the dream.
One tree can start a forest, One bird can herald spring.
One smile begins a friendship, One handclasp lifts a soul.
One star can guide a ship at sea, One word can frame the goal.
One vote can change a nation, One sunbeam lights a room.
One candle wipes out darkness, One laugh will conquer gloom.
One step must start each journey, One word must start each prayer.
One hope will raise our spirits, One touch can show you care.
One voice can speak with wisdom, One heart can know what's true.
One life can make the difference, You see it's up to YOU!

Positive People Power

Don't ever forget how very important YOU are.

Every morning in Africa a gazelle wakes up.
It knows it must run faster than the fastest lion or it will be killed.
Every morning a lion wakes up also.
It knows that it must out run the slowest gazelle or it will starve to death.
It doesn't matter whether you are a lion or a gazelle.
When the sun comes up, YOU HAD BETTER BE RUNNING !!!

The longer I live, the more I realize the impact of attitude on life. Attitude, to me, is more important than fact. It is more important than the past, than education, than money, than circumstances, than failures, than successes, than what other people say or do.
It is more important than appearances, giftedness or skill.
It will make or break a company...a church...a home.
The remarkable thing is we have a choice everyday regarding the attitude we embrace for that day.
We can not change our past. The only thing we can do is play on the one string we have, and that is attitude.
I am convinced that life is 10% what happens to me and 90% how I react to it.

People leave their jobs for many reasons. Often it's a better opportunity elsewhere or a better paycheck. However, even with the lure of more money, most people who are reasonably content with their work and their leaders seldom go looking for other jobs.
Sometimes, obviously, people have been offered opportunities and salaries which are so extraordinary that all you could have done in any case is to let them go and wish them well. But, don't be too sure.

Positive People Power

Before you let yourself off the hook, ask yourself a few questions and answer them as honestly as you can.

* Did I let these people know how important they were to me and to the company? Or did I more or less take them for granted?

* Did I give them chances to be proud of themselves? Did I pass along all the authority I possibly could - or keep them tied to a string?

* Did I give these people - and get for them - the credit and recognition they deserved from me and from others up the line? Or did I tend to leave them in the shadows?

* Were the jobs challenging to them? Did I do my best to make them so?

* Did I make their work as varied and interesting as possible? Did I show them the possibilities of promising futures? Or did I simply leave them in ruts and exploit their abilities to my own advantage?

If you were responsible, in any respect, for their leaving, it's smarter to realize it than to hide your head in the sand. Unless you change your attitude or actions, you may lose more good people for the same reasons. The best time to think of these things is before you lose good people rather than after.

This philosophy applies to managers, supervisors, team leaders, committee chairs, not only in business, but in any organization, club, association, or volunteer group you may be involved in. Give people the recognition, applause, responsibility for jobs well done and you will have happy employees, members and real contributors to whatever your goals, dreams, hopes and ambitions may be.

The length of your life is not as important as the quality of your life.
-Zorba

Positive People Power

Life is what you do after you're born while you're waiting to die, so put some of the following into action and make your waiting more fun and productive.

Concentrate on making others like and enjoy themselves, they'll enjoy you more.

Give others the benefit of the doubt, and doubt often-emphasize the benefit.

Forget your ability to think faster than another person talks ... everybody has it, but only the foolish use it. When you're thinking ahead, you can't hear what's being said.

Listen at least twice as much as you talk...others will hear twice as much as you say.

Laugh with others often...only fools never laugh, or laugh at others.

Use plain talk...say what you mean, precisely what you mean, and only what you mean.

Ask for more advice than you give...the wise seek counsel and the foolish only give it.

Criticize sparingly, and then only constructively...one compliment is always worth a dozen critical remarks.

Be approachable...few people talk often to a dragon, or a stone wall or a ghost.

Positive People Power

Seek to know others...you'll be amazed at how it will help you understand yourself.

Greet every person you meet cheerfully and enthusiastically...nobody can fake cheerfulness and enthusiasm very long. You'll either quit trying or improve your outlook.

Leave every person feeling better for having talked to you...they'll be happy to see you next time.

Human beings are the only creatures on earth that allow their children to come back home. - Bill Cosby

If you want work well done, select a busy man; the other kind has no time. - Elbert Hubbard

Your education begins when what you call your education ends. - Oliver Wendell Holmes

Luck is what you have left over after you give 100%.
- Langston Coleman

The only time you mustn't fail is the last time you try.
 - Charles Kettering

A successful man is one who can lay a firm foundation with the bricks that others throw at him. - David Brinkley

Recent events have caused me to assess television news from a different perspective. Too often we get caught in the negative news syndrome - the first 10 -15 minutes of almost every national and local television newscast is devoted to the worst events or crimes in the city and country. My philosophy is that the reason they show this - is that it really is the news, the extraordinary, the unusual, the exceptional.

Because most folks like you and me got up this morning and did the right things, took time for our families, provided service to our customers, all with a positive attitude.

So I believe as long as they show the exceptional bad news, then this country is in good shape.

Think about it - If they ever start showing 10-15 minutes of good news - then that would mean the good is the unusual, the extraordinary and the exceptional - and that would be a real cause for concern.

When elections come, please be aware of the issues and informed about the candidates, because you can affect the following situation that too often involves us.

SOMETHING ELSE TO THINK ABOUT: THE LAWS OF THE LAND

My shattered financial situation is due to the federal laws, state laws, county laws, city laws, corporation laws, law-making bodies, mothers-in-law, sisters-in-law, brothers-in-law, and out-laws.

Through laws I am compelled to pay business tax, amusement tax, head tax, bank tax, income tax, food tax, furniture tax, excise tax, gasoline tax, beer tax, environmental tax, vehicle tax, a tax to live, a tax to die and then inheritance tax. I am required to get a business license, hunting license, fishing license, a car license, and a dog license.

I am also required to contribute to every society and organization which the genius of man is capable of bringing into existence, to give relief to unemployed, the indisposed, plus the gold diggers relief; also to every hospital and charitable institution, including the Red Cross, Blue Cross and double cross.

For my own safety, I am required to carry life insurance, property insurance, liability insurance, burglary insurance, accident insurance, medical insurance, windstorm, flood and fire insurance.

My business is so governed that it is no easy matter to find out who owns what. I am expected, inspected, suspected, disrespected, examined, re-examined, informed, required, summoned, condemned and compelled, until I provide inexhaustible supply of money and reports for every known need, desire or hope of the human race.

And simply because I refuse to donate to something or other, I am boycotted, talked about, lied about, held up, held down, and robbed until I am almost ruined.

This check which I enclose could not have happened but for a miracle. The wolf that comes to many doors nowadays had pups in my kitchen. I sold them and here is the money. (I will probably receive a protest from the wolf lovers association).

While the above letter is taken to extremes, it should make us wonder how much encroachment on our freedom is needed until we say "no more"; until we force a political appraisal by those who, claiming to care about us, actually put us in a bind. Your vote is important in coming elections.

The man who steps into a cage with a dozen lions impresses everybody except a school-bus driver.

In youth we want to change the world; in old age we want to change youth. - Bob Brown

Positive People Power

The only thing that keeps a man going is energy. And what is energy but liking life! - Louis Auchincloss

The following are from the book, *You Can If You Think You Can* by Norman Vincent Peale.

1. Believe that you have inherent in your mind all the resources you will ever need.
2. Build up your resources inventory by faith and know-how.
3. Remember that spiritual power activates your forces of mind and spirit.
4. Never minimize your ability to think your way through any situation.
5. If power isn't coming through, find the block and remove it.
6. Keep alert for those flashes of insight which come when you're really thinking.
7. Skip "if only"; concentrate on "next time."
8. Never bog down in a defeat psychology. Always, in the midst of defeat, keep looking for victory.
9. Be bold, and mighty powers will come to your aid.
10. The tests of life are to make, not break you. And nothing can break you when you have going for you the powerful resources of your mind.

Faith is broadcasting good news to yourself: "I am alive! I survived the night. I did not die in my sleep. I have been given free-of-charge the gift of another day, fresh and clean. It affords me wonderful and marvelous opportunities to think, plan, execute, advance, build, love and enjoy. Tune your mental dial into radio station TGNT - There's Good News Today.

A troubled man made an appointment with a rabbi. He was a wise and gentle rabbi. "Rabbi," said the man, wringing his hands. "I'm a failure. More than half the time I do not succeed in doing what I know I must."

"Oh," murmured the rabbi.

"Please tell me what I should do," pleaded the man.

After much pondering the rabbi replied, "Ah, my son, I give you this bit of wisdom: go and look on page 930 of The New York Times Almanac for the year 1970, and maybe you will find peace of mind." Confused by such strange advice, the troubled man went to the library to look up the source. And this is what he found - lifetime batting averages for the world's greatest baseball players. Ty Cobb, the greatest slugger of them all, had a lifetime average of .367. Even the King of Swat, Babe Ruth, didn't do that well.

So the man returned to the rabbi and questioned, "Ty Cobb, .367. That's it?"

"Correct," countered the rabbi. "Ty Cobb, .367. He got a hit once out of every three times at bat. He didn't even hit .500. So what do you expect already?"

"Aha," said the man, who thought he was a wretched failure because he only succeeded half the time at what he must do.

Theology is amazing. Holy books abound, even where we don't expect them.

At election time, you might enjoy the following before you go and vote.

HOW TAX LAWS ARE MADE

We recently had the opportunity to hear about tax changes and prospects in the future. It's such an accurate description of how tax law is made that it hurts.

In the beginning was the Act. Then the Regulations and Interpretations. And the Act was without form and the Interpretations were vague. And Darkness was upon the faces of the Taxpayers. And they spoke unto the Civil Servant saying, "It is a crock of s... and it stinketh."

And the Civil Servant went to the Manager saying, "It is a crock of excrement. And none may abide its odor."

And the Manager went to the Commissioner saying, "It is a container of excrement. And is very strong. Such that all are stunned by it."

And the Commissioner went before the local member of Congress saying, "It is a vessel of fertilizer. And none may stand before its strength."

And the Local Member of Congress went before the Joint Committee on taxation saying, "It contains that which aids plant growth. And it is very strong."

And the Joint Committee went before the House of Representatives and Senate saying, "It promotes growth and it is powerful."

And the House of Representatives and the Senate went before the President saying,
" This powerful new law will promote employment and reduce the deficit."

And the President looked upon the law and saw that it was good.
And so it was written.

Discipline is the refining fire by which talent becomes ability.
- Roy L. Smith

Positive People Power

There is no comparison between that which is lost by not succeeding and that which is lost by not trying. - Francis Bacon

To dislike learning is to dislike living, and children who reject education are complaining more about their lives than about their schools - although both may be bad. - John M. Henry

A SUMMARY OF THE WORLD

If we could shrink the Earth's population to a village of precisely 100 people with all the existing human ratios remaining the same, it would look like this:

* There would be 57 Asians, 21 Europeans, 14 from North and South America, and 8 Africans.
* 51 would be female; 49 would be male.
* 70 would be non-white; 30 would be white.
* 70 would be non-Christian; 30 would be Christian.
* 50% of the world's wealth would be in the hands of only 6 people, and all 6 people would be from the United States.
* 80 would live in substandard housing.
* 70 would be unable to read.
* 50 would suffer from malnutrition.
* One would be near death; one would be near birth.
* Only one would have a college education.
* No one would own a computer.

When one considers our world from such an incredibly compressed perspective, the need for both tolerance and understanding becomes glaringly apparent.   (Unknown)

Positive People Power

From the wit and wisdom of Will Rogers:
If you want to be successful it's just this simple,
Know what you are doing.
Love what you are doing.
And believe in what you are doing.

In our approach to knowledge we must realize that preparation is a constant with no ending. It must be forever moving, never static. School is never out for the person who really wants to succeed. There is no saturation point.

Knowledge is accumulating so fast and methods of doing things improving so rapidly that a person today must run to stand still.

Nothing takes a greater toll on us than to be around a pessimist - a person always finding fault and criticizing others. We've all seen the type. He has mental B.O. He's a one man grievance committee, always in session. He criticizes everyone and everything.
You ask him, "How is business?" and he says, "Well, I made a sale on Monday. I didn't sell anything Tuesday. Wednesday the deal I made on Monday fell through - so, I guess Tuesday was really my best day."

Persuasion is converting people - no, not to our way of thinking, but to our way of feeling and believing.

People are persuaded more by the depth of your conviction than by the height of your logic - more by your enthusiasm than any proof you can offer.

Ordinary people believe only in the possible. Extraordinary people visualize not what is possible or probable, but rather what is impossible. And by visualizing the impossible, they begin to see it as possible. - Cherie Carter-Scott

Vision without action is merely a dream. Action without vision just passes time. Vision without action can change the world. A true leader must first see an idea as opportunity, then choose to act upon it. - Joel Barker

"We are most like beasts when we kill.
We are most like men when we judge.
We are most like God when we forgive."

Dr. Victor E. Frankl, a survivor of three grim years at Auschwitz and other Nazi prisons, recorded the following observations on life in these camps:

"We who lived in Hitler's concentration camps can remember the men who walked through the huts comforting others, giving away their last piece of bread. They have been few in number, but they offer sufficient proof that everything can be taken from a man but one thing: the last of human freedoms - to choose one's attitude in any given set of circumstances, to choose one's own way."

"Therefore I say to you, do not worry about your life, what you will eat or what you will drink; nor about your body, what you will put on. Is not life more than food and the body more than clothing?...for your Father knows that you need all these things."
- Matt. 6:25,32

In my life, I have found there are two things about which I should never worry. First, I shouldn't worry about the things I can't change.

If I can't change them, worry is certainly most foolish and useless. Second, I shouldn't worry about the things I can change. If I can change them, then taking action will accomplish far more than wasting my energies in worry. Besides, it is my belief that, 9 times out of 10, worrying about something does more danger that the thing itself. Give worry its rightful place - out of your life.
- Source Unknown

An anagram, as we all know, is a word or phrase made by transposing or rearranging the letters of another word or phrase. The following examples are quite astounding:
Dormitory = Dirty Room
Desperation = A Rope Ends It
The Morse Code = Here Come Dots
Slot Machines = Cash Lost in 'em
Snooze Alarms = Alas! No More Z's
Alec Guinness = Genuine Class
The Public Art Galleries = Large Picture Halls, I Bet
A Decimal Point = I'm a Dot in Place
The Earthquakes = That Queer Shake
Eleven plus two = Twelve plus one
Contradiction = Accord not in it

According to the late and dearly beloved, Og Mandino, the book that has probably had the greatest impact on personal success is Napoleon Hill's, THINK AND GROW RICH. This book contains so much practical and easy-to-follow advice. When you read this book you should have pen or hi-lighter in your hand because you will want to underline, hi-light, circle, use stars, exclamation marks or any other attention-getter you choose in order to help you plant specific ideas in your brain that you believe will help you achieve your goal.

Following are a few highlights that will hopefully whet your appetite to read this classic.

* Purpose is the touchstone of any accomplishment, large or small. A strong man can be defeated by a child who has purpose. Shift your habits of thinking about the significance of your task and you can often accomplish the seemingly impossible.

* Both poverty and riches are the offspring of faith.

* Success requires no explanations. Failure permits no alibis.

* Opportunity has spread its wares before you. Step up to the front, select what you want, create your plan, put the plan into action, and follow through with persistence. Capitalistic America will do the rest. You can depend upon this much...capitalistic America insures every person the opportunity to render useful service and to collect riches in proportion to the value of the service.

* Remember that every time you open your mouth in the presence of a person who has an abundance of knowledge, you display to that person your exact stock of knowledge or your lack of it. Genuine wisdom is usually conspicuous through modesty and silence.

* The world has a habit of making room for the man whose words and actions show that he knows where he is going.

* The starting point of all achievement is desire. Keep this constantly in mind. Weak desires bring weak results, just as a small amount of fire makes a small amount of heat. If you find yourself lacking in persistence, this weakness may be remedied by building a stronger fire under your desires.

* Poverty is attracted to the one whose mind is favorable to it, as money is attracted to him whose mind has been deliberately prepared to attract it, and through the same laws.

* Too many people refuse to set high goals for themselves or even neglect selecting a career because they fear the criticism of relatives

and friends who may say, "Don't aim so high, people will think you are crazy."
* It is necessary to plan and to organize in order to get rich. Staying poor is very easy; poverty needs no plan.
* Sex energy is the creative energy of all geniuses. There never has been, and never will be, a great leader, builder, or artist lacking in this driving force.
* Beyond your own mind lies an Infinite Intelligence to which your mind can be tuned like a radio set, both sending and receiving. The energy of the entire universe can help your prayers be answered.

Napoleon Hill was often criticized for his apparent concentration on wealth as the ultimate goal; however, this criticism nearly always came from individuals who had read his works superficially. Actually, Napoleon Hill was not pro-wealth as much as he was anti-poverty. He wrote: "the fear of poverty is, without a doubt, the most destructive of man's fears. Nothing brings man so much suffering and humiliation as poverty! Only those who have experienced poverty understand the full meaning of this."

Afraid of poverty? Get yourself a copy of THINK AND GROW RICH.

Politeness is the hallmark of the gentle-man and the gentle-woman. No characteristic will so help one to advance, whether in business or society, as politeness. Competition is so keen today, there is so much standardized merchandise, there are so many places where one's wants can be supplied, that the success or failure of a business can depend on the ability to please customers or clients. Courtesy - another name for politeness - cost nothing, but can gain much for both an individual and for an organization. - B. C. Forbes

Positive People Power

To a young man on the flying trapeze a veteran circus performer once said: "Throw your heart over the bars and your body will follow." In every field of endeavor those who put their hearts in their work are the real leaders. Falling in love with one's job is the secret of success.

It has been said of athletes that they are only as good as their last game. Unless a career has been completed, yesterday's success may be lost by today's failure. This, likewise, applies to all men of accomplishment. - Frederick Lobi

This generation is not given to dreaming elaborate dreams but to enacting modest ones. Without visionaries who ponder endless schemes for saving the world, they set themselves to the tasks at hand. The difference between our generation and theirs is, as one sociologist explains, that the younger generation has turned all the nouns into verbs. - David O. Woodyard

Men do less than they ought, unless they do all that they can.
 - Thomas Carlyle

A good deed is never lost; he who sows courtesy, reaps friendships; and he who plants kindness, gathers love. - Richard Brooks

Never stand begging for that which you have the power to earn. - Cervantes

Fear not that thy life shall come to an end, but rather fear that it shall never have a beginning. - Cardinal Newman

If your foot slips you may recover your balance, but if your tongue slips you cannot recall your words. - Martin Vanbee

Positive People Power

A true talent will make do with any technique. - Eric Hoffer

Wondrous is the strength of cheerfulness, and its power of endurance. The cheerful man will do more in the same time, will do it better, will persevere in it longer, than the sad or sullen. - Thomas Carlyle

The world belongs to the energetic. - Emerson

Sympathy is never wasted except when you give it to yourself.
- John W. Raper

Diligence is the mother of good luck. - Benjamin Franklin

I believe in work, hard work, and long hours of work. Men do not break down from overwork, but from worry and dissipation.
- Charles Evans Hughes

The high minded man does not bear grudges, for it is not the mark of a great soul to remember injuries, but to forget them. - Aristotle

When Charles Lindbergh left New York for Paris in his plane, The Spirit of St. Louis, on May 12, 1927, he risked failure, at least in the eyes of the world. Significantly, however, Lindbergh believed fervently that he would reach Paris safely. He know every nut and bolt and every wire in his plane, and he believed in his own competence. When he arrived in Paris he said for himself and his plane, "We did it."
It is faith, deep faith in a dream, that makes the impossible dream possible, and faith makes us willing to accept the possibility of failure. Robert Frost spoke for all the dreamers of impossible dreams when he wrote: "You're always believing ahead of your evidence.

What was the evidence I could write a poem? I just believed it. The most creative thing in us is to believe a thing in...You believe yourself into existence...Your marriage. I believe the future in. It's coming in by my believing it. You might as well call that belief in God."
Let there be no mistake, those who are willing to risk the possibility of failure are "always believing ahead of" the "evidence."

Success
Scenes

**"It is every man's obligation
to put back into the world
at least the equivalent of
what he takes out of it.
- Albert Einstein**

Those who fashioned our Declaration of Independence believed ahead of their evidence. "We hold these truths to be self-evident," they wrote. "That all men are created equal; that they are endowed by their creator with certain inalienable rights; that among these are life, liberty, and the pursuit of happiness." However, there is nothing self-evident about the rights affirmed or the equality announced in the great Declaration. They were affirmations of faith and hope, nothing more nor less. What is more, whatever progress we have made toward implementing the "inalienable rights" proclaimed by those who signed the document in Independence Hall has been made possible by those who refused to believe in the impossibility of their impossible dream.

Every great thing that has been undertaken by the dreamers of dreams has been ventured at the risk of failure. The Wright brothers had no guarantee that they could fly. They simply believed that could. Those who dreamed of putting men on the moon had no insurance against failure. They believe they could do it, and they did. No business ever was planned and built without the risk of failure, a risk accepted on the intangible belief it could be done. - Harold Blake Walker

If one advances confidently in the direction of his dreams, and endeavors to live the life which he imagined, he will meet with a success unexpected in common hours...in proportion as he simplifies his life, the laws of the universe will appear less complex, and solitude will not be solitude, nor poverty poverty, nor weakness weakness. If you have built castles in the air, your work need not be lost; that is where they should be. Now put foundations under them. - Henry David Thoreau

Here's a way to help build up someone's sense of confidence. Ask them to fold a sheet of paper in half and make two parallel lists: *Strengths* on one side and *Weaknesses* on the other.

Ask them which list was easier to create and which was longer. (People who lack confidence will invariable find it easier to come up with a list of weaknesses.)

Remind them that successful people build on their strengths, rather than focusing on their weaknesses (which they have like anyone else.) People who fail are governed by <u>attitudes based on their weaknesses.</u> Ask how their lives might change if they focused only on their strengths and stopped dwelling on their weaknesses. They'll discover for themselves the positive people power that lies within each of us.

It's a cheery old world when you're cheerful,
And a glad old world when you're glad.
but whether you play or go toiling away
It's a sad old world when you're sad.

It's a grand old world when you're great
And a mean old world when you're small,
It's a world full of hate for the foolish who prate
On the usefulness of it all.

It's a beautiful world to see,
Or it's dismal in every zone,
The thing it must be in its gloom or its gleam
Depends on yourself alone.
- Author Unknown

When we look into the long avenue of the future, and see the good there is for each one of us to do, we realize, after all, what a beautiful thing it is to work, and to live, and to be happy.
- Robert Louis Stevenson

What's the most important technique for turning yourself into an outstanding public speaker? Public speaking instructor Dorothy Leeds says it's this: "Analyze your strengths and build on them."
If you're lively and energetic, build those qualities into your speech.
If you're very sincere about your topic, stress that.
If you're comfortable asking questions or taking questions from the audience, do that.
In her speech training courses, when Leeds gives a group of ten students an assignment to sell her a pencil, they usually come up with ten entirely different solutions-that's how unique we all are!
Individuals aren't only unique in their faces and fingerprints, but in how they move, use gestures, interpret information, tell stories and use timing. Even our voices differ.
So being yourself is the most important and worthwhile thing you can do to come across effectively.

You can make more friends in two months by becoming really interested in other people than you can in two years by trying to get other people interested in you. - Dale Carnegie

The Lord gave you two ends - one for sitting and one for thinking. Your success depends on which one you use - heads you win, tails you lose. - Anonymous

VINCE LOMBARDI'S CREDO FOR SUCCESS

Winning is not a sometime thing; it's an all-the-time thing. You don't win once in a while. You don't do things right once in a while. You do them right all the time. Winning is a habit. Unfortunately, so is losing.

There is no room for second place. There is only one place in my game and that is first place. I have finished second twice in my time at Green Bay, and I don't ever want to finish second again. There is a second place bowl game, but it is a game for losers played by losers. It is and always has been American zeal to be first in anything we do and to win and to win and to win.

Every time a football player goes out to ply his trade, he's got to play from the ground up - from the soles of his feet right up to his head. Every inch of him has to play. Some guys play with their heads. That's okay. You've got to play smart to be No. 1 in any business. But more important, you've got to play with your heart - with every fiber of your body. If you're lucky enough to find a guy with a lot of head and a lot of heart, he's never going to come off the field second.

Running a football team is no different from running any other kind of organization - an army, a political party, a business. The principles are the same. The object is to win - to beat the other guy. Maybe that sounds hard or cruel. I don't think it is.

It's a reality of life that men are competitive and the most competitive games draw the most competitive men. That's why they're there - to compete. They know the rules and the objectives when they get in the game. The objective is to win - fairly, squarely, decently, by the rules - but to win.

And in truth, I've never known a man worth his salt who in the long run, deep down in his heart, didn't appreciate the grind, the discipline. There is something in good men that really yearns for, needs: discipline and the harsh reality of head-to-head combat.

97

I don't say these things because I believe in the "brute" nature of man or that men must be brutalized to be combative. I believe in God, and I believe in human decency. But I firmly believe that any man's finest hour - his greatest fulfillment to all he holds dear - is that moment when he has worked his heart out in a good cause and lies exhausted on the field of battle - victorious.

What you are will show in what you do. - Thomas A. Edison

When you judge another, you do not define them, you define yourself. - Wayne Dyer

You're never a loser until you quit trying. - Mike Ditka, Coach

Even a happy life cannot be without a measure of darkness, and the word happy would lose its meaning if it were not balanced by sadness. It is far better to take things as they come along with patience and equanimity. - Carl Jung

If there is light in the soul, there will be beauty in the person.
If there is beauty in the person, there will be harmony in the house.
If there is harmony in the house, there will be order in the nation.
If there is order in the nation, there will be peace in the world.
- Chinese Proverb

Only I can change my life. No one can do it for me. - Carol Burnett

A winner is someone who recognizes his God-given talents, works his tail off to develop them into skills, and uses these skills to accomplish his goals. - Larry Bird

SNOWFLAKE
YOU CAN MAKE A DIFFERENCE...

"Tell me the weight of a snowflake" a sparrow asked a wild dove.

"Nothing more than nothing," was the answer.

"In that case I must tell you a marvelous story," the sparrow said.

"I sat on the branch of a fir next to its trunk. It began to snow - not heavily. I counted the snowflakes settling on the twigs and needles of my branch. Their number was 3,741,952. When the next snowflake fell - nothing more than nothing, the branch broke off."

The sparrow flew away.

The dove thought about it and said, "Perhaps there is only one person's voice lacking for peace to come about in the world."

NEVER DISCOUNT YOUR INFLUENCE,
YOUR PRESENCE,
YOUR VALUE.
YOU COUNT !!!

After a forest fire in Yellowstone National Park, forest rangers began their trek up a mountain to assess the inferno's damage. One ranger found a bird literally petrified in ashes, perched statuesquely on the ground at the base of a tree.

Somewhat sickened by the eerie sight, he knocked over the bird with a stick. When he struck it, three tiny chicks scurried from under their dead mother's wings. The loving mother, keenly aware of impending disaster, had carried her offspring to the base of the tree and had gathered them under her wings, instinctively knowing that the toxic smoke would rise. She could have flown to safety but had refused to abandon her babies. When the blaze had arrived and the heat had singed her small body, the mother remained steadfast. Because she had been willing to die, those under the cover of her wings would live.

"He shall cover thee with His feathers, and under His wings shalt thou trust." (Psalm 91:4) - Author Unknown

You are not judged by the things you do at Christmas, but by the Christmas things you do all year long.

My dog is worried about the economy because Alpo is up to 99 cents a can. That's about $7.00 in dog money. - Joe Weinstein

AND THEN SOME

A retired business executive said it, "I discovered at an early age that most of the differences between average people and top people could be explained in these three words - "and them some." By the phrase "and then some," he meant people were more thoughtful of others, they were more considerate - "and then some." They met their obligations and responsibilities fairly, squarely, on time - "and then some."

Of the many quotes made by the late World Heavyweight Boxing Champion, James J, Corbett, during his colorful career, one was preeminent. When asked by a reporter what was most important for a man to become a champion, Corbett replied, "Fight one more round."

This was Jim Corbett's way of saying, "and then some."

100

You remember that the Lord Jesus asked his followers the test question, "What do ye more than others?"

We have our heroes and we find that most of these who have excelled could be identified by the three words, "and then some."

Thomas Edison, seeking a proper filament to light his incandescent lamp, failed month after month; but one day his efforts were successful. The world was presented with the electric light. He knew the meaning of "and then some."

S.N. Behrman, one of America's outstanding playwrights, turned out manuscripts for eleven years before he finally sold his first play - "and then some."

Fannie Hurst wrote more than 100 stories before one was ever accepted - "and then some."

Somerset Maugham was a failure for ten years, earning five hundred dollars in all that time. A producer hard put for a play dug out the forgotten manuscript, "Lady Fredrick," and Maugham became the toast of London - "and then some."

We have become computerized workers who are clock watchers. There is no romance in working overtime nor is there any reason we shouldn't leave on time. But if you measure your performance by the clock, it usually indicates just getting by with the least effort. Personal satisfaction comes when we leave knowing we've put forth the extra effort.

For some unexplainable reason, many projects are successful when someone has felt he could and then he gives it that one more effort - the finest tradition of "and then some."

GET OUT OF THAT RUT

Oscar Wilde said, "Consistency is the last refuge of the unimaginative." So stop getting up at 6:05. Get up a 5:06. Walk a mile at dawn. Find a new way to drive to work. Switch chores with your spouse next Saturday. Buy a wok. Study wildflowers. Stay up alone all night. Read to the blind. Subscribe to an out-of-town newspaper. Canoe at midnight. Don't write your congressman, take a whole scout troop to see him. Learn to speak Italian. Teach some kid the thing you do best. Listen to two hours of uninterrupted Mozart. Take up aerobic dancing. Leap out of that rut. Savor life. Remember, we only pass this way once.

We judge ourselves by what we feel capable of doing, while others judge us by what we have already done.
 - Henry Wadsworth Longfellow

I was watching some little kids play soccer. These kids were only five or six years old, but they were playing a real game - - a serious game - two teams, complete with coaches, uniforms, and parents. I didn't know any of them, so I was able to enjoy the game without the distraction of being anxious about winning or losing - I wished the parents and coaches could have done the same.
The teams were pretty evenly matched. I will just call them Team One and Team Two. Nobody scored in the first period. The kids were hilarious. They were clumsy and terribly inefficient. They fell over their own feet, they stumbled over the ball, they kicked at the ball and missed it but they didn't seem to care. They were having fun.

In the second quarter, the Team One coach pulled out what must have been his first team and put in the scrubs, except for his best player who now guarded the goal. The game took a dramatic turn. I guess winning is important even when you're five years old -- because the Team Two coach left his best players in, and the Team One scrubs were no match for them. Team Two swarmed around the little guy who was now the Team One goalie. He was an outstanding athlete, but he was no match for three or four who were also very good. Team Two began to score. The lone goalie gave it everything he had, recklessly throwing his body in front of incoming balls, trying valiantly to stop them. Team Two scored two goals in quick succession. It infuriated the young boy. He became a raging maniac -- shouting, running, diving. With all the stamina he could muster, he covered the boy who now had the ball, but that boy kicked it to another boy twenty feet away, and by the time he repositioned himself, it was too late -- they scored a third goal.

I soon learned who the goalie's parents were. They were nice, decent-looking people. I could tell that his dad had just come from the office -- he still had his suit and tie on. They yelled encouragement to their son. I became totally absorbed, watching the boy on the field and his parents on the sidelines.

After the third goal, the little kid changed. He could see it was no use; he couldn't stop them. He didn't quit, but he became quietly desperate; futility was written all over him.

His father changed too. He had been urging his son to try harder - yelling advice and encouragement. But then he changed. He became anxious. He tried to say that it was okay - to hang in there. He grieved for the pain his son was feeling.

After the fourth goal, I knew what was going to happen. I've seen it before. The little boy needed help so badly, and there was no help to be had. He retrieved the ball from the net and handed to the referee - and then he cried. He just stood there while huge tears rolled down both cheeks. He went to his knees and put his fists to his eyes - and he cried the tears of the helpless and brokenhearted.
When the boy went to his knees, I saw the father start onto the field. His wife clutched his arm and said, "Jim, don't. You'll embarrass him." But he tore loose from her and ran onto the field. He wasn't

supposed to - the game was still in progress. Suit, tie, dress shoes, and all - he charged onto the field, and he picked up his son so everybody would know that this was his boy, and he hugged him and held him and cried with him. I've never been so proud of a man in my life.

He carried him off the field, and when he got close to the sidelines I heard him say, "Scotty, I'm so proud of you. You were great out there. I want everybody to know that you are my son."
"Daddy," the boy sobbed, "I couldn't stop them. I tried, Daddy, I tried and tried, and they scored on me."

"Scotty, it doesn't matter how many times they scored on you. You're my son, and I'm proud of you. I want you to go back out there and finish the game. I know you want to quit, but you can't. And, son, you're going to get scored on again, but it doesn't matter. Go on, now."
It made a difference - I could tell it did. When you're all alone, and you're getting scored on - and you can't stop them - it means a lot to know that it doesn't matter to those who love you. The little guy ran back on to the field - and they scored two more times - but it was okay.

I get scored on every day. I try so hard. I recklessly throw my body in every direction. I fume and rage. I struggle with temptation and sin with every ounce of my being - and Satan laughs. And he scores again, and the tears come, and I go to my knees - sinful, convicted, helpless. And my Father - my Father rushes right out on the field - right in front of the whole crowd - the whole jeering, laughing world - and he picks me up, and he hugs me and he says, "John, I'm so proud of you. You were great out there. I want everybody to know that you are my son, and because I control the outcome of this game, I declare you -- The Winner."

WHY MOTHERS CRY...
"Why are you crying?" he asked his mom.
"Because I am a mother," she told him.
"I don't understand," he said.
His mom just hugged him and said, "You never will..."
Later the boy asked his father why Mother seemed to cry for no reason.
"All mothers cry for no reason," was all his dad could say.

The little boy grew up and became a man, still wondering why mothers cry. So finally he put a call in to God and asked, "God, why do mothers cry so easily?"

The Lord replied, "You see son, when I made mothers they had to be special. I made their shoulders strong enough to carry the weight of the world, yet gentle enough to give comfort. I gave them an inner strength to endure childbirth and the rejection that many times comes from their children."

"I gave them a hardiness that allows them to keep going when everyone else gives up, and to take care of their families through sickness and fatigue without complaining. I gave them the sensitivity to love their children under all circumstances, even when their child has hurt them very badly. This same sensitivity helps them to make a child's boo-boo feel better and helps them share a teenager's anxieties and fears."

"I gave to them a tear to shed. It is theirs exclusively to use whenever it is needed. It is their only weakness. It is a tear for mankind."

"THE NORDSTROM WAY" - Nordstrom's Department Store employee's handbook is just a five-by-eight-inch gray card that reads: We're glad to have you with our company. Our number one goal is to provide outstanding customer service. Set both your personal and professional goals high. We have great confidence in your ability to achieve them.

Rule #1: Use your good judgment in all situations. There will be no additional rules. Please feel free to ask your department manager, store manager, or division general manager any question at any time.

MAKE THE MOST OF YOUR CIRCUMSTANCES.

Sooner or later a crisis appears in your life, and how you meet it will determine your future happiness and success.

Since the beginning of time, everyone has been called upon to meet such a crisis.

Close examination will show you that most "crisis situations" are opportunities to either advance or stay where you are.

Indeed most changes in your life seem to be due to either "inspiration" or "desperation".

Your personal growth is the process of responding positively to change.

Give whatever comes your way meaning and transform it into something of value.

A precious stone cannot be polished without friction, nor humanity perfected without trials.

The secret of life is not to do what you like, but to like what you do.
The more you study, the more you find out you don't know,
but the more you study, the closer you come. - Cozy Cole

You can't have everything. Where would you put it? - Steven Wright

24 Things to Always Remember by: Collin McCarty
Your presence is a present to the world.
You're unique and one of a kind.
Your life can be what you want it to be.
Take the days just one at a time.

Count your blessings, not your troubles.
You'll make it through whatever comes along.
Within you are so many answers.
Understand, have courage, be strong.

Don't put limits on yourself.
So many dreams are waiting to be realized.
Decisions are too important to leave to chance.
Reach for your peak, your goal, your prize.

Nothing wastes more energy than worrying.
The longer one carries a problem, the heavier it gets.
Don't take things too seriously.
Live a life of serenity, not a life of regrets.

Remember that a little love goes a long way
Remember that a lot...goes forever.
Remember that friendship is a wise investment.
Life's treasures are people...together.

Realize that it's never too late.
Do ordinary things in an extraordinary way.
Have health and hope and happiness.
Take time to wish upon a star.
And don't ever forget...for even a day...how very special you are.

Yes, you can be a dreamer and a doer too, if you will remove one word from your vocabulary: Impossible. - Robert Schuller

C'mon Guys
I know it isn't Valentine's Day yet, but, whether you are a husband, boyfriend, significant other, friend, or even just single, quit waiting for a holiday as an excuse to do some of the following for your special person:

Go for a walk and hold their hand.

Don't take more out of your relationship than you put in.

Cook for them when they are sick.

Get out of the bed first on cold mornings and turn up the heat.

Only the strongest men are gentle.

Don't put your special person on a pedestal, they don't want to be that far away.

If you feel empty when they are away, tell them when they get back.

Remember she married you - so don't ask her to be logical.

Pray together.

If she can't start the lawnmower, blame it on the mower.

Always ask her to dance.

Watch a sunset together - in silence.

She is your partner - so stand up for her.

Flirt with her once in a while.

While she is in the shower, warm her bath towel in the dryer.

Worship together.

If you can give your son or daughter only one gift, let it be enthusiasm. - Bruce Barton

The only thing that makes one place more attractive to me than another is the quantity of heart I find in it. - Jane Welsh Carlyle

THOUGHTS OF A WINNER!!!

Although I am only one out of a million, I am somebody, and that makes me as good as the next person.

There is nothing in this life I cannot do. There is no goal I cannot tackle and, have success. If I feel deep down inside that something is important to me, then I can do it. If my mind can conceive it and believe it then I know I can achieve it. No longer will I drift through life feeling sorry for myself, because self-pity is the seed of destruction.

I will search for a goal, and with enough hard work, total commitment, determination, dedication, and self-sacrifice, I know I will reach it. I know there will be many times when it will seem that all the odds are against me, and I will have to fight one battle after another - **but I will not give up!** - Author Unknown

INK IT!

Until I am solidly committed, I write in pencil. But then comes the time when I either erase or write in INK! That's the point of commitment. Faith is inking the agreement. It's the pouring of cement!

Irrevocable commitments that offer no loopholes, or no bail-out provisions extract incredible productivity and performance.

Inking an agreement is making a commitment to continuity.

- Dr. Robert Schuller

YOU ARE THE MASTER OF YOUR FATE.

It is your philosophical set of the sails
that determines the course of your life.

To change your current direction,
you have to change your philosophy not your circumstances.

109

Instead of saying, "I sure hope things will change".
Learn that the only way things are going to change is when you change.

Disgust and resolve are two of the great emotions that lead to change.
You will generally change yourself for one of two reasons:
Inspiration or Desperation

Don't say, "If I could, I would".
Say instead, "If I can, I will ".

There is nothing so absurd or ridiculous that has not at some time been said by some philosopher. - Oliver Goldsmith

Let us so live that when we come to die even the undertaker will be sorry. - Mark Twain

Part of the secret of success in life is to eat what you like and let the food fight it out inside. - Mark Twain

There is a story about a lumberjack who started his job and cut down 10 trees his first day, 15 trees his second day until by the end of the week, he was cutting down 25 trees in one day. When he started he was given a brand new ax. By the time the second week started, he was very experienced but he started to notice something that began to frustrate him. He was able to cut 25 trees but was more fatigued by the end of the day. By the end of the second week he was no longer cutting 25 trees per day but was down to 20. By the beginning of the third week, he was working even harder and cutting even less per day.

He went in to see the foreman, having become totally frustrated. The foreman asked him to show him the ax he was using. Upon presenting the ax, the foreman noticed how dull the edge was. The foreman asked him why he allowed the ax to become so dull. The lumberjack replied that he was so busy trying to cut his 25 trees per day, he didn't have time to sharpen his ax.

Isn't that like most of us, whether we are lumberjacks, business people, educators, students or creative individuals - when we lose our edge, we aren't as productive. The POSITIVE PEOPLE POWER! Newsletter is like a sharpening stone for the ax; it sharpens our minds and gives us the edge we need to perform at our best.

If you think you are too busy to investigate the benefits that POSITIVE PEOPLE POWER! can provide to your organization, remember the lumberjack who was so busy cutting that he had no time to sharpen his ax. He lost his edge...don't lose yours.

SUCCESSFUL ACTION IS CUMULATIVE IN ITS RESULTS.

All masters of success are chiefly distinguished
by their power of adding a second, a third,
and perhaps a fourth step in a continuous line.
Many people have taken the first step and then stop.
With every additional step you take,
you enhance immensely the value of your first step.
Success is the sum of small efforts,
repeated day in and day out.
There is no royal road to anything.

One thing at a time, all things in succession.
That which grows fast, withers as rapidly.
That which grows slowly, endures.
Do not despise the bottom rungs in your ascent to greatness.

ONLY IN AMERICA

Only in America...can a pizza get to your house faster than
an ambulance...

Only in America...do we leave cars worth thousands of dollars in
the driveway and leave useless things and junk in boxes in the
garage...

Only in America...do banks leave both doors open and then
chain the pens to the counters...

Only in America...do we use answering machines to screen calls
and then have call waiting so we won't miss a call from someone
we didn't want to talk to in the first place...

Men do less than they ought, unless they do all that they can.
 - Thomas Carlyle

THE OPTIMIST vs. THE PESSIMIST

The optimist turns the impossible into the possible; the pessimist turns
the possible into the impossible.
The optimist pleasantly ponders how high his kite will fly; the
pessimist woefully wonders how soon his kite will fall.
The optimist sees a green near every sand trap; the pessimist sees a
sand trap near every green.
The optimist looks at the horizon and sees an opportunity; the
pessimist peers into the distance and fears a problem.

The optimist promotes progress, prosperity, and plenty; the pessimist preaches limitations, liabilities, and losses.

The optimist accentuates assets, abundance, and advantages; the pessimist majors in mistakes, misfortunes, and misery.

The optimist goes out and finds the bell; the pessimist gives up and wrings his hands. - William Arthur Ward

I am a New Day. I come to you pure and unstained, fresh from the hand of God. Each day, a precious pearl to you is given that you must string upon the silver thread of life. Once strung, it can never be unthreaded, but it stays an undying record of your faith and skill. Each golden minute links you then must weld into the chain of hours that is no stronger than its weakest link. Into your hands is given all the wealth and power to make your life what you will. I give to you, free and unstilted, every day, glorious moments of work and play. All that I have, I give with love unspoken. All that I ask - you keep the faith unbroken. - Anonymous

Right is right, even if everyone is against it; and wrong is wrong, even if everyone is for it. - William Penn

Disturb us, O Lord

Disturb us, O Lord, when we are too well pleased with ourselves; when our dreams have come true because we dreamed too little, when we have arrived in safety because we sailed close to the shore.

Disturb us, O Lord, when with the abundance of things which we possess we have lost our thirst for the water of life.

Stir us, O Lord, to dream and dare more boldly, to venture on wider seas where storms shall show Thy master, where losing sight of land we shall find the stars. Amen.

American Character

Americanism means the virtues of courage, honor, justice, truth, sincerity and hardihood-the virtues that made America great. The things that will destroy America are prosperity-at-any-price, safety first instead of duty first, the love of soft living and the get-rich-quick theory of life. - Theodore Roosevelt

Never exaggerate your faults. Your friends will attend to that.
- Robert C. Edwards

Spread love everywhere you go: first of all in your own house. Give love to your children, to your wife or husband, to a next door neighbor or friends. Let no one ever come to you without leaving better and happier. Be the living expression of God's kindness; kindness in your face, kindness in your eyes, kindness in your smile, kindness in your warm greeting. - Mother Teresa

In the spirit of Mother Teresa, let's pass on hugs this week.

Hugs

It's wondrous what a hug can do.
A hug can cheer you when you're blue,
a hug can say, "I love you so"
or, "Gee, I hate to see you go."
A hug is "welcome back again,"
and, "great to see you! Where've you been?"
A hug can soothe a small child's pain
and bring a rainbow after rain.

114

The hug! There's just no doubt about it -
we scarcely could survive without it.
A hug delights and warms and charms.
It must be why God gave us arms.
Hugs are great for fathers and mothers,
sweet for sisters, swell for brothers,
and chances are your favorite aunts
love them more than potted plants.
Kittens crave them, puppies love them.
Heads of state are not above them.
A hug can break the language barrier
and make your travels so much merrier.
No need to fret about your store of 'em,
the more you give, the more there's more of 'em.
So stretch those arms without delay,
and give someone a hug today!

HUGGING - THE PERFECT CURE
FOR WHAT AILS YOU !

HUGGING IS HEALTHY
IT RELIEVES TENSION
COMBATS DEPRESSION
REDUCES STRESS
IMPROVES BLOOD CIRCULATION
IT'S INVIGORATING
IT'S REJUVENATING
IT ELEVATES SELF-ESTEEM
IT GENERATES GOODWILL
IT HAS NO MOVABLE PARTS
NO BATTERIES TO WEAR OUT
LOW ENERGY CONSUMPTION

HIGH ENERGY YIELD
INFLATION-PROOF
THEFT-PROOF
NON-TAXABLE
NON-POLLUTING
NO MONTHLY PAYMENTS
NO INSURANCE REQUIREMENTS
NO PERIODIC CHECKUPS
NO UNPLEASANT SIDE EFFECTS
IT IS NOTHING LESS THAN A MIRACLE DRUG
AND, OF COURSE, FULLY RETURNABLE.

This is the beginning of a new day. God has given me this day to use as I will. I can waste it - or use it for good, but what I do today is important because I am exchanging a day of my life for it! When tomorrow comes, this day will be gone forever, leaving in its place something that I have traded for it. I want it to be gain, and not loss; good, and not evil; success, and not failure; in order that I shall not regret the price that I have paid for it.
- D. Heartsill Wilson

If you do not hope, you will not find what is beyond your hopes.
- St. Clement of Alexandria

SUCCESS
It's doing your job the best you can,
And being just to your fellow man.
It's figuring how, and learning why
And looking forward and thinking high.
And dreaming little and doing much:
It's keeping always in closest touch
With what is finest in word and deed:

116

It's being clean, and it's playing fair:
It's laughing lightly at dame despair;
It's sharing sorrow, and work, and mirth.
And making better this good old earth:
It's serving and striving through strain and stress
It's doing your noblest - that's success.   - Unknown

HOW MUCH ARE YOU WORTH?

Your real worth is not in what you have, but in what you are, and what is recognized by your services to those who need them.

The worthy whose worth excel all riches are those who live for others. More worthy than the self-indulgent are the self-giving. More praise worthy than being good is doing good. More valuable than glory is a good name.

As you give you'll get what you gave.   Recompense for your benevolent gifts is a gladdened heart and gratifying remembrances.

You are worth only what you are good for.

How much are you worth as your brother's keeper?

How much are you worth as an example to youth?

How much are you worth as a friend to the friendless?

How much are you worth as a fighter of adversities?

How much are you worth as an inspiration to the despairing?

How much are you worth as a solace to the grieved?

How much are you really worth to the world about you?

How much were you worth, to how many, today?

-- Joseph Evans

You know if a man had a bank that credited his account each morning with $86,400, but carried over no balance from day to day, allowed him to keep no cash in his account and every evening, canceled out whatever part of that amount he failed to use during the day.....what

117

do you think he would do? He probably draw out every cent, every day...wouldn't you???
Well, every man does have such a bank and its' name is "time".
Every morning you are credited with 86,400 seconds . Every night, the bank rules as lost whatever of this you have failed to invest to good purposes! You carry over no balance and no overdrafts are allowed. If you fail to use the day's deposit, the loss is yours. There is no going back. No drawing against tomorrow. So you need to invest your seconds in the priorities that will give you the utmost in health, happiness and success.
What is a day worth to you?
What did you do with your day today?
What will you do with your day tomorrow?

Have you heard of the man who didn't have time?
He hadn't time to greet the day, he hadn't time to laugh or play;
He hadn't time to wait a while, he hadn't time to glean the news,
he hadn't time to dream or muse;
He hadn't time to train his mind; he hadn't time to see a joke,
he hadn't time to write his folks;
He hadn't time to eat a meal, he hadn't time to deeply feel,
He hadn't time to take a rest, he hadn't time to do his best;
He hadn't time to help a cause, he hadn't time to make a pause;
He hadn't time to pen a note, he hadn't time to cast a vote;
He hadn't time to sing a song, he hadn't time to right a wrong;
He hadn't time to send a gift, he hadn't time to practice thrift;
He hadn't time to exercise, he hadn't time to say good-bye;
He hadn't time to study poise, he hadn't time to repress noise;
He hadn't time to serve his God;
He hadn't time to lend or give, he hadn't time to really live;
He hadn't time to read this verse,
He hadn't time - he's in a hearse - he's dead.

TAKE TIME
You know it's never too late to be what you could have been.
So, Take time to work; it is the price of success.
Take time to think; it is the source of power.
Take time to play; it is the secret of youth.
Take time to read; it is the foundation of wisdom.
Take time to laugh; it is the music of the soul.
Take time to be friendly; it is the road to happiness.
Take time to dream; it is the highway to the stars.
Take time to look around; it is the shortcut to unselfishness.
Take time to pray; it is the way to Heaven.

THE DASH
I read of a man who stood to speak at the funeral of his friend.
He referred to the dates on her tombstone from the beginning...to the end.
He noted that first came the date of her birth, he spoke of the second with tears,
but he said that what mattered most of all was the dash between those years.
For that dash represents all the time that she spent alive on earth,
and now only those who loved her know what that little line is worth.
For it matters not, how much we own; the cars, the house, the cash.
What matters is how we live and love and how we spend our dash.
So think about this long and hard, are there things you'd like to change?
For you never know how much time is left. (You could be at "mid-dash range.")
If we could just slow down enough to consider what's true and real,
and always try to understand the way other people feel.
And...be less quick to anger, and show appreciation more
and love the people in our lives like we've never loved before.

If we treat each other with respect, and more often wear a smile,
remembering that this special dash might only last a little while.
So, when your eulogy is being read with your life's actions to rehash...
Would you be pleased with the things that they say about...how you
spent your dash?

THE LEGEND OF THE EASTER EGG
One day a poor peddler went to the marketplace to sell a basket of
eggs.
He came upon a crowd mocking a man who staggered with a heavy
cross on which he was about to be crucified.
The peddler ran to his aid, leaving the basket by the roadside.
When he returned, he found the eggs transformed into exquisite
designs of bright colors.
The man was Christ; the peddler, Simon.
And the eggs were to become the symbol of rebirth for all mankind.
- UKRAINIAN FOLK TALE

The best vitamin for making friends: B-one.

CHOICES
You are where you want to be right now because of all you do and say
and every choice you've made in life has brought you to this day.
They say that life is choice and this I know is true, and if you do not
make a choice, the choice is made for you.
So don't complain about your life and say there's nothing you can do
for anything you choose in life will surely come to you.

IT'S ALWAYS YOUR NEXT MOVE.
The keys to your universe lie with the choices you make.
You don't have to buy from anyone.
You don't have to work at any particular job.

You don't have to participate in any given relationship.
The choice is always yours.
You hold the tiller.
You steer the course you choose in the direction of where you want
to be today, tomorrow, or in a distant time to come.
You can at any time decide to alter the course of your life.
No one can take that away from you.
You can choose.

Most people never run far enough on their first wind to find out
they've got a second. Give your dreams all you've got and you'll be
amazed at the energy that comes out of you. - William James

GOLFER'S GRACE
Dear Lord, life is not unlike a game of golf, and in a lifetime one
plays many courses. In our formative years we were pretty new to the
game. Oh, but those early courses held much excitement, despite for
some of us the Great Depression. We remember them well - school,
courtship, first love, first job and for some, college. Then three really
tough courses had to be mastered, World War II, Korea and Vietnam.
These matured our game considerably for the challenges ahead.
Chances and changes influenced our choices. And yes, we chose the
courses, and are accountable. Some were easy: others, fraught with
traps, hazards and narrow fairways. But you showed us the way, and
we are grateful.
Now, retired in relative comfort and security, we often play the same
familiar course. Yet even so, mistakes are made. Sometimes we
underclub and come up short - we lack empathy or understanding, a
memorable event is forgotten, or a deserving compliment, thank you,
"I'm sorry," or apology is left unsaid. And at other times we overclub
with equal hurt, with a strong bias, a superior, self-righteous, or
uncompromising attitude, or perhaps just by a harsh word or

unintentional rebuke. For these failings we beg your forgiveness and that of those we've injured.

Heavenly Father, you have been our faithful and trusted caddie for oh, these many years. We pray that with your continued guidance we can keep in the fairway through life's passage, and that all our troubles will be short putts. Amen.

Keep on going and the chances are you will stumble on something, perhaps when you are least expecting it. I have never heard of anyone stumbling on something sitting down.
 - Charles F. Kettering

All my life I used to wonder what I would become when I grew up. Then, about seven years ago, I realized that I was never going to grow up - that growing is an ever ongoing process. - M. Scott Peck

YOU ARE SURROUNDED BY OPPORTUNITY.
The people that really succeed in the world are the people who get up and look for the circumstances they want, and, if they can't find them, make them.
The lure of the distant and the difficult is deceptive.
The great opportunity in your life is where you are right now.
Properly perceived, every situation becomes an opportunity for you.
Your destiny is not a matter of chance, it is a matter of your choice.
It is not something you wait for, but rather something you achieve with effort.
Things won't turn up in this world until you turn them up.
You develop opportunity by applying persistence to your possibilities.
Opportunity is all around you.
Look for it, and you will find it.

It is better to be a part of a great whole than to be the whole of a small part. - Frederick Douglass

Perhaps the most insidious level you can reach is when you take your competence for granted - when you no longer have to scramble to do well. You just have to show up, go through the motions, and produce what you have produced for longer than you care to remember. The condition seems even more worrisome than burning out, for living on a reputation not only insults your own talents but it also drags down just about everybody around you. Indeed, you may not have burned out, but you are hardly burning.
You worry that you will never again get a good idea. Or just an idea. You worry that you'll never again be awakened in the dead of night by a creative surge, one caused by an inspiration instead of by a full bladder.
You realize that the dread of burning out is within anyone who has ever made a success, written a song, met a quota, fallen in love, been consumed. Burning out, then, is so much more trivial than never having been ignited. - William Brashler

Fortunate are the persons,
Who in this life can find
A purpose that can fill their days,
And goals to fill their minds!

The world is filled with many people,
Content with where they are;
Not knowing joys success can bring,
No will to go that far.

Yet in this world there is a need
For people to lead the rest,

123

To rise above the "average" life,
By giving of their best!

Would you be the one who dares to try
When challenged by the task?
To rise to heights you've never seen,
Or is that too much to ask?

This is your day - a world to win,
Great purpose to achieve
Accept the challenges of your goals
And in yourself believe!!!!   - Anonymous

Think excitement, talk excitement, act out excitement and you are bound to become an excited person. Life will take on a new zest, deeper interest and greater meaning. - Norman Vincent Peale

Five Fun, Fantastic Things to Accomplish in Your Lifetime!!!
1. Learn to say the alphabet backward.
2. Be on the cover of *Time*
3. Visit the house where you were born.
4. Blow soap bubbles in the office.
5. Wine and dine someone who deserves it.

I'm just a plowhand from Arkansas, but I have learned how to hold a team together. How to lift some men up, and how to calm down others, until finally they've got one heartbeat together, a team. There's just three thing I'd ever say:
* If anything goes bad, I did it.
* If anything goes semi-good, then we did it.
* If anything goes real good, then you did it.

That's all it takes to get people to win football games for you.
- Bear Bryant

Humor is something that causes a tickling of the brain. Laughter is invented to scratch it. - Hugh Foot

Walking to the front of the classroom, a young boy desired to give his teacher a gift that represented the special feelings of love he had for her. He stopped at the front at the front of her desk a bit nervous, for he did not know whether she would treasure the tiny seashell that he clutched in his hand. With extended arms, the young boy not only showed his teacher the special seashell, but also a portion of his heart. Upon seeing the gift the teacher knew then how hard the young boy had labored to get this special seashell. She knew how far away the beach was and how long the walk was to obtain such a shell. It was a very rare present. Hard to find. Precious. A radiant red. Small in size...yet infinite in expression. It was a beautiful shell.
The teacher held out her hand as the young boy placed the small shell in her palm...
"For you," he replied.
She could not understand as to why he had gone to such great lengths to obtain such a gift. It was not expensive. It was not elaborate. Yet special. She asked him, "Why did you walk so far, so long, and put forth so much labor for just one seashell?"
To her question he replied, "Ma'am the walk was part of the gift."
Every step...Every moment...Every thought was all part of the gift.
- Author Unknown

The more faith you have the more you believe,
The more goals you set the more you'll achieve.
So reach for the stars, pick a mountain to climb,

Dare to think big, but give yourself time.
Remember no matter how futile things seem.
With faith, there is no Impossible Dream. - Author Unknown

Instead of giving someone a piece of your mind, give them a piece of your positive attitude.

The only real mistake is the one from which we learn nothing.
 - John Enoch Powell

The world is divided into people who do things and people who get the credit. Try, if you can, to belong to the first class. There's far less competition. – Dwight Whitney Morrow

Terrific
Touchstones

"Some people see things
as they are and say, "Why?"
I dream of things that never were
and say, "Why not?"
George Bernard Shaw

127

WHO PACKED YOUR PARACHUTE?

Sometimes in the daily challenges that life gives us, we miss what is really important. We may fail to say hello, please, or thank you, congratulate someone on something wonderful that has happened to them, give a compliment, or just do something nice for no reason.

Charles Plumb, a US Naval Academy graduate, was a jet pilot in Vietnam. After 75 combat missions, his plane was shot down by a surface-to-air missile. Plumb ejected and parachuted into enemy hands. He was captured and spent 6 years in a communist Vietnamese prison. He survived the ordeal and now lectures on lessons learned from that experience.

One day, when Plumb and his wife were sitting in a restaurant, a man at another table came up and said, "you're Plumb! You flew jet fighters in Vietnam from the aircraft carrier Kitty Hawk, You were shot down!"

"How in the world did you know that?" asked Plumb. "I packed your parachute," the man replied. Plumb gasped in surprise and gratitude. The man pumped his hand and said "I guess it worked!".

Plumb assured him "It sure did. If your chute hadn't worked, I wouldn't be here today."

Plumb couldn't sleep that night, thinking about that man. Plumb says, "I kept wondering what he might have looked like in a Navy uniform: A white hat, a bib in the back, and bell bottom trousers. I wonder how many times I might have seen him and not even said good morning, how are you, or anything, you see, I was a fighter pilot and he was just a sailor." Plumb thought of the many hours the sailor had spent on a long wooden table in the bowels of the ship, carefully

128

weaving the shrouds and folding the silks of each chute, holding in his hands each time the fate of someone he didn't know.

Now Plumb asks his audiences, "Who's packing your parachute?" Everyone has someone who provides what they need to make it through the day." Plumb also points out that he needed many kinds of parachutes when his plane was shot down over enemy territory. He needed his physical parachute, his mental parachute, his emotional parachute, and his spiritual parachute. He called on all of these supports before reaching safety.

His experience reminds us all to prepare ourselves to weather whatever storms lie ahead. As you go through this week, this month, this year recognize the people who pack your parachute!

You've got to get up every morning with a smile on your face and show the world all the love in your heart. Then people are going to treat you better. You're going to find, yes you will, that you're beautiful as you feel. - Carole King

* I believe the single most significant decision I can make on a day to day basis is "my choice of attitude." It is more important than my past, my education, my bankroll, my successes or failures, fame or pain, what other people think about me, or say about me, my circumstances or my position.

Attitude is that "single string" that keeps me going or cripples my progress. It alone fuels my fire or assaults my hope. When my attitudes are right there's no barrier too high, no valley too deep, no dream too extreme, no challenge too great for me!

The following was found hanging in a OB/Gyn doctor's office:
"The Meanest Mother"
I had the meanest mother in the whole world. While other kids ate candy for breakfast, I had to have cereal, eggs, and toast. When

129

others had cokes and candy for lunch, I had to eat a sandwich. As you can guess my supper was different from the other kids' too, but, at least I wasn't alone in my sufferings. My sister and two brothers had the same mean mother as I did.

My mother insisted on knowing where we were at all times. You'd think we were on a chain gang. She had to know who our friends were and what we were doing. She insisted if we said we'd be gone an hour that we'd be gone an hour or less--not one hour and one minute. I am nearly ashamed to admit it, but she actually struck us-- not once, but each time we did as we pleased. Can you imagine someone actually hitting a child just because he disobeyed? Now you can begin to see how mean she really was.

The worst is yet to come. We had to be in bed by nine each night and up early the next morning. We couldn't sleep till noon like our friends, so while they slept my mother actually had the nerve to break the child labor law. She made us work. We had to wash dishes, make beds, learn to cook, and all sorts of cruel things. I believe she laid awake at night thinking up mean things to do to us.

She always insisted upon our telling the truth, the whole truth, and nothing but the truth, even if it killed us--and it nearly did.

By the time we were teenagers she was much wiser, and our life became even more unbearable. None of this tooting the horn of a car for us to come running. She embarrassed us to no end by making our dates and friends come to the door to get us. I forgot to mention, while my friends were dating at the mature age of 12 and 13, my old-fashioned mother refused to let me date until the age of 15 and 18. Fifteen, that is, if you dared only to go to school functions and that was maybe twice a year.

My mother was a complete failure as a mother. None of us has ever been arrested, divorced, or beaten his mate. Each of my brothers served his time in the service of his country. And whom do we have to blame for the terrible way we turned out? You're right, our mean

130

mother. Look at all the things we missed. We never got to march in a protest parade, nor take part in a riot, burn draft cards, and a million and one things our friends did. She forced us to grow up into God-fearing, educated, honest adults.

Using this as a background, I am trying to raise my three children. I stand a little taller and I am filled with pride when my children call me mean. Because, you see, I thank God. He gave me the meanest mother in the world.

RICH LADY/ POOR LADY

They huddled inside the storm door - two children in ragged outgrown coats.

"Any old papers, lady?"

I was busy. I wanted to say no - until I looked down at their feet. Thin little sandals, sopped with sleet. "Come in and I'll make you a cup of hot cocoa." There was no conversation. Their soggy sandals left marks upon the hearthstone. I served them cocoa and toast with jam to fortify against the chill outside. Then I went back into the kitchen and started again on my household budget...The silence in the front room struck through to me. I looked in.

The girl held the empty cup in her hands, looking at it.

The boy asked in a flat voice, "Lady...are you rich?"

"Am I rich? Mercy, no!" I looked at my shabby slip covers.

The girl put her cup back in its saucer - carefully.

"Your cups match your saucers." Her voice was old, with a hunger that was not of the stomach.

They left then, holding their bundles of papers against the wind. They hadn't said thank you. They didn't need to.

They had done more than that. Plain blue pottery cups and saucers. But they matched. I tested the potatoes and stirred the gravy, a roof over our heads, my man with a good steady job - these things matched, too.

I moved the chairs back from the fire and tidied the living room. The muddy prints of small sandals were still wet upon my hearth. I left them there, I want them there in case I ever forget how very rich I am.
- Marion Doolan

The secret of getting ahead is getting started. The secret of getting started is breaking your complex overwhelming tasks into small manageable tasks, and then starting on the first one. - Mark Twain

A COURSE IN TIME MANAGEMENT
One day an expert in time management was speaking to a group of business students and, to drive home a point, used an illustration those students will never forget. As he stood in front of the group of high powered overachievers he said, "Okay, time for a quiz."
Then he pulled out a one gallon, wide mouth mason jar and set it on the table in front of him. Then he produced about a dozen fist sized rocks and carefully placed them, one at a time, into the jar.
When the jar was filled to the top and no more rocks would fit inside, he asked, "Is this jar full?"
Everyone in the class said, "Yes."
Then he said, "Really?" He reached under the table and pulled out a bucket of gravel. Then he dumped some gravel in and shook the jar causing pieces of gravel to work themselves down into the space between the big rocks.
Then he asked the group once more, "Is the jar full?"
By this time the class was on to him. "Probably not," one of them answered.
"Good!" he replied. He reached under the table and brought out a bucket of sand. He started dumping the sand in the jar and it went into all of the spaces left between the rocks and the gravel. Once more he asked the question, "Is this jar full?"
"No!" the class shouted.

Once again he said, "Good."
Then he grabbed a pitcher of water and began to pour it in until the jar was filled to
the brim. Then he looked at the class and asked, "What is the point of this illustration?"
One eager beaver raised his hand and said, "The point is, no matter how full your schedule is, if you try really hard you can always fit some more things in it!"
"No," the speaker replied, "that's not the point.
The truth this illustration teaches us is: If you don't put the big rocks in first, you'll never get them in at all."
What are the 'big rocks' in your life? Time with your loved ones?
Your faith, your education, your dreams? A worthy cause? Teaching or mentoring others? Remember to put these BIG ROCKS in first or you'll never get them in at all.
So, tonight, or in the morning, when you are reflecting on this short story, ask yourself this question: What are the 'big rocks' in my life? Then, put those in your jar first.

Success is the sum of small efforts -- repeated day in and day out.
- Robert Collier

Tomorrow's success is the result of today's planning. Failing to plan is planning to fail. You can't increase your time, but you can increase the value of your time. Master the success habit of managing your time more effectively. Also, learn to identify signs of procrastination or "Someday I'll" syndrome. Develop a mind-set that judges your every activity in terms of whether it brings you closer to your goals. Most people get ahead during the time others waste. Let the minutes of each day count in your favor.

Time is the most valuable thing a man can spend. - Diogenes

133

The following story relates to the American Legion (war veterans) who every year sell paper poppies to commemorate the sacrifices many made to freedom of the world. On May 31, Memorial Day, buy a poppy and understand and know from whence the tradition originated - Lest we forget those who gave!!!

*The Poppy Legend originated in China. A white flower from which a potent drug was distilled was called The Flower of Forgetfulness. Genghis Kahn brought some of the seed westward but after a battle the flower became red. In the center of each was a cross.

It was found that on many battlefields, when everything else had been laid waste, the landscape was soon ablaze with the blood-red blooms. On the Somme battlefield in 1917 (and again after the war was over), the land burst forth in a blaze of scarlet with patches of yellow charlock and white chamomile. Many graves of those buried near the front line were soon marked by the poppy due to the seeds being released when the graves were dug.

In 1915, during the second battle of Ypres, Canadian solider and physician Lt. Col. John McCrea wrote a poem called "In Flanders Fields". In the poem, he mentions the poppies that grow in a field that was the site of a bloody battle. The poem was published anonymously in England's Punch Magazine's December 8, 1915 issue. McCrea died of pneumonia January 28, 1918 -- months before large-scale fighting took place in the Flanders area.

The brief verse caught the imagination of England, American and, of France. The poppy -- long the traditional flower of sleep - became an emblem of the Allied Dead. When peace came the bright field flower already typified the bravery and sacrifice of the war. It had been worn in honor of the dead before the war closed.

On Armistice Day, November 9, 1918, Miss Monica Michael, of Athens Georgia, was a worker for the Y.M.C.A. at its Overseas Headquarters at the Hamilton Hall, Columbia University. On that day a soldier gave a copy of The Ladies Home Journal containing Colonel John McCrea's poem to her. She read it and was deeply impressed. She was moved to write a poem of her own in reply, expressing the feeling of the living, as Colonel McCrea's had supposedly expressed that of the dead.

As she finished the last lines, a committee from the 25th conference of the YMCA which was meeting upstairs, brought her a check for $10 in appreciation of having made the meeting room attractive with flowers.. "How strange that you should bring me this gift at this time!" she exclaimed. "And," she continued, "I shall buy with it bright red poppies - Flanders Field poppies. Do you know why?" She showed them the poem and her answer.

She proceeded to buy the poppies (which were easily available) and meanwhile the men with whom she had talked told the conference upstairs of her idea. Men coming from the conference stopped at her office and got poppies to wear. As far as is known, this was the first conscious and formal use of the flower in America.

Miss Michael returned to Georgia and brought her idea to the Georgia Dept. convention which met on August 18, 1920. The poppy was adopted as the Department flower -- the first adoption by a Legion Department. And the Convention instructed its delegates to the imminent Cleveland Convention on September 27th to propose the poppy as The American Legion's flower. It was adopted and The American Legion was the first organization to do so.

For it isn't enough to talk about peace. One must believe in it. And it isn't easy to believe in it. One must work at it. - Eleanor Roosevelt

Within ourselves are the seeds of triumph or defeat. - Longfellow

A group of frogs were traveling through the woods, and two of them fell into a deep pit. All the other frogs gathered around the pit.
When they saw how deep the pit was, they told the two frogs that they were as good as dead. The two frogs ignored the comments and tried to jump out of the pit with all of their might. The group of frogs kept telling them to stop because they were as good as dead.
Finally, one of the frogs took heed to what the other frogs were saying and gave up. He fell down and died. The second frog continued to jump as hard as he could. Once again, the crowd of frogs yelled at him to stop the pain and just die. He jumped even harder and finally made it out.
You see this frog was deaf, unable to hear what the others were saying. He thought they were encouraging him the entire time.
This story teaches a lesson.... Proverbs 18:21
There is the power of life and death in the tongue. An encouraging word to someone who is down can lift them up and help them make it through the day. A destructive word to someone who is down can be what it takes to kill them. Be careful of what you say. Speak life to those who cross your path. The power of words...an encouraging word can go such a long way. May your words be a blessing to someone today!

RULES FOR BEING HUMAN
You will receive a body. You may like it or hate it, but it will be yours for as long as you live. How you take care of it can make an enormous difference in the quality of your life.

136

You will learn lessons. Each day you will presented with opportunities to learn what you need to know. The lessons presented are often completely different from those you think you need.

There are no mistakes - only lessons. Growth is a process of trial and error and experimentation. You can learn as much from failure as you can from success.

A lesson will be presented to you in various forms until you have learned it. When you have learned it, then you can go on to the next lesson. Learning lessons does not end. As long as you live, there will be something more to learn.

"There" is no better than "here". When your "there" has become a "here", you will obtain another "there" that will again look better than your "here". Don't be fooled by believing that the unattainable is better than what you have.

Others are merely mirrors of you. You cannot love or hate something about another person unless it reflects something you love or hate about yourself. When tempted to criticize others, ask yourself why you feel so strongly.

What you make of your life is up to you. You have all the tools and resources you need. Remember that through desire, goal-setting and unflagging effort you can have anything you want.

The solution to all of life's problems lie within your grasp. All you need to do is ask, look, listen and trust.

You will forget all this, unless you consistently stay focused on the goals you have set for yourself. If you don't stay focused then everything you've just read won't mean a thing.
- Cherie Carter - Scott PhD

Those on top of the mountain did not fall there. - Unknown

Worldwide competition provides the United States with a major reason to improve performance. We attribute others' success to low wages, but there are other factors.

About 72 percent of all U.S. students graduate from high schools. 92 percent in West Germany. And 13 percent of all Americans are illiterate compared to 5 percent in Japan. Japanese students attend school 240 days a year. Korean children 250 days, and U.S. students 180 days. Also, U.S. firms invest much less time in training.

In his book, Peak Performers, business writer Charles Garfield say U.S. firms must:
1. Decide to excel
2. Learn from setbacks
3. Sustain commitment
4. Define individual and team missions
5. Build group pride
6. Seek individual excellence
7. Persist even when goals seem unreachable
8. Put restlessness to work
9. Integrate natural talents and acquired skills
10. Pay attention to preferences

"You cannot strengthen the weak by weakening the strong. You cannot help the wage earner by pulling down the wage payer. You cannot help the poor by destroying the rich. You cannot help men permanently by doing for them what they could and should do for themselves." - John Henry Boetker

YOUR MIND IS YOUR LIMIT.
The only thing that stands between you and what you want from life is simply your will to try it and the faith to believe that it is possible.

138

Your mind will amaze your body. You must find the energy and determination to keep going. Keep telling yourself, you can do it, you can do it. When you believe you can, you can.

In belief there is power. It opens your eyes, your opportunities become plain, and your vision becomes reality. You will succeed when you believe you can succeed. The only limit to your realization of tomorrow will be your doubts of today.

Many great things are accomplished in absolute silence. Although a chorus of sounds accompanies nature, the soundless wonders never cease. The sun rises - and the sun sets. Stars twinkle - and the moon shines. Magnificent happenings without sound.
Bud to blossom - blossom to fruit - fruit to seed - seed to sprout - sprout to branch - branch to bud - silent pulsating energy.
The ripening of June hangs heavily in fruit and pods, and on ears, maturing in silent achievement.
Nature is a kaleidoscope of quiet beauty - iridescent dewdrops sparkling in the grass, frosty filigrees on a window pane and veils of mist and fog suspended from the clouds. Rainbows arch across the heavens and snow drapes the hillside.
Some activities are even silent - spiders spinning a web, snakes slithering in the grass, butterflies dancing in the garden and eagles soaring high overhead.
Nature's silent wonders surround us they bathe us in pre-dawn glory and soothe us in the afterglow of sunset. The magnificent silent wonders of God's Creation. - Joanne Walker

All the wonders you seek are within yourself. - Sir Thomas Brown

WHAT IS A GOAL?

A goal is a target, a point of completion for a predetermined desire or want, a place where we can see if our intentions are being realized. Our minds want to see the light at the end of the tunnel. It is extremely difficult for us to get motivated about making any progress towards an unknown target. Without the target, we tend to stop progressing and just exist. We tend to drift aimlessly, just taking what comes our way.

A goal does not need to be a physical object or wealth. A goal is anything we want - any thing, any action, any condition, any experience, quality in our lives.

Goals are wants, desires, dreams, things we'd like to see in ourselves, in our lives, and in our environment.

Goals are truly personal. They are declarations of our own personal intentions in life. Goals can also be professional, if that is what we personally desire. Goals can be set for our own internal sense of ourselves. Goals can be set for how we relate to others. Goals can be set for how we want others to relate to us. Goals can be expressed for the kind of person we want to be. Goals can be expressed for the things we want to have. Goals can be expressed for what we want to do.

Goals are a vital part of who we are. Goals are our own personal aims and targets that we want for ourselves, even though it sometimes looks like we want them for others.

Goals are the fuel of a satisfying life. To have no goal is like running out of gas and being parked on the planet like an abandoned car, waiting to be towed away. Why not make life as interesting, as challenging, as satisfying as you can? Why not express your goals? Why not get them all out there so you have a full tank of gas, so that you are fully energized?

We must never be afraid to go too far, for success lies just beyond. - Marcel Proust

Charles Sykes is the author of DUMBING DOWN OUR KIDS.
He volunteered for high school and college graduates a list of eleven things they did not learn in school. In his book, he talks about how the <u>feel-good, politically-correct teachings</u> created a generation of kids with no concept of reality and set them up for failure in the real world. You may want to share this list with them.

Rule 1: Life is not fair; get used to it.

Rule 2: The world won't care about your self-esteem. The world will expect you to accomplish something BEFORE you feel good about yourself.

Rule 3: You will NOT make 40 thousand dollars a year right out of high school. You won't be a vice president with a car phone until you earn both.

Rule 4: If you think your teacher is tough, wait till you get a boss. He doesn't have tenure.

Rule 5: Flipping burgers is not beneath your dignity. Your grandparents had a different word for burger flipping; they called it opportunity.

Rule 6: If you mess up, it's not your parents' fault, so don't whine about your mistakes. Learn from them.

Rule 7: Before you were born, your parents weren't as boring as they are now. They got that way from paying your bills, cleaning your clothes, and listening to you talk about how cool you are. So before you save the rain forest from the parasites of your parents' generation, try delousing the closet in your own room.

Rule 8: Your school may have done away with winners and losers but life has not. In some schools they have abolished failing grades; they'll give you as many times as you want to get the right answer.

This, of course, doesn't bear the slightest resemblance to ANYTHING in real life.

Rule 9: Life is not divided into semesters. You don't get summers off, and very few employers are interested in helping you find yourself. Do that on your own time.

Rule 10: Television is NOT real life. In real life people actually have to leave the coffee shop and go to jobs.

Rule 11: Be nice to nerds. Chances are you'll end up working for one.

What you want to be eventually you must be every day. With practice, the quality of your deeds will get down into your soul.
   - Frank Crane

THE MUSTARD SEED

As the ancient Chinese parable unfolds we are introduced to a woman who has suffered inexplicable pain. Her only son received a wicked, violent and wholly unjust mortal wound. By his fatality she is crushed. In the fog of her pain she violates a cultural taboo by soliciting the local holy man to resurrect her son by magical incantation.

The holy man was unwilling to expose his limitations, yet he neither reasoned with her nor summarily sent her away. He could not raise the boy, so he sent the mother on a fanatical search with these words, "Fetch me a mustard seed from a home that has never known sorrow. With it we will create a potion and drive sorrow from your life." Thus the journey began.

The grief stricken woman approached a mansion. It's facade was immaculate. It's lawn manicured. "Surely a home as beautiful as this has never met with pain," she reasoned. The door opened to her knock. She explained herself to the greeter, concluding her tale with these words, "...so I have been commissioned to find a house that has never known sorrow. Is this such a place? May I have a mustard seed from you?"

"This is not such a place," was the reply. The greeter told his own painful tale to the woman. He, too, would like to have a seed from such a place once she found it. As the woman heard his words she listened with her heart and reasoned within, "Who is better able to minister to this poor soul than I, for he has suffered the same misfortunes as I." Thus she stayed and counseled.

When she resumed her search she found the same story across the land. The details changed from home to home. For some it was financial loss. Others lost love in death or infidelity. Still more told stories of failing health, inadequate help, betrayal and disappointment. The details changed but the pain was the same. Each home had been touched by an injustice. Each home deserved better. Each home silently grieved.

From shack to chandeliered palace she was greeted with tale after sad tale. Soon she found herself so caught up ministering to the pain of others that she forgot about the search for the mustard seed, never realizing that it had, in fact, driven the sorrow from her life.

Discovery lies in seeing what everyone sees, but thinking what no one else has thought.

At first people refuse to believe that a strange new thing can be done, and then they begin to hope it can be done, and then they see it can be done - then it is done and all the world wonders why it was not done centuries ago. - Frances Hodgson Burnett

FUN THINGS TO DO!!!
- Develop your own chili recipe
- Say things like "eureka", "balderdash", and "hallelujah"

- Eat your vegetables
- Hang a spoon from your nose
- Take everything off your desk and start over
- Get involved

Our care should not be to have lived long, but to have lived long enough. - Seneca

Everyone has pride and love for their own country and for Americans there is much pride and love, along with and in spite of, the many negative things that happen here. Too many times I've heard people ask the wrong question. They say "what's wrong with America?" When the question they should be asking is "what's right with America?" and then how do we improve on the right things and go about making it even better.

Before he died, John Wayne recorded several songs about America. Here is one that was written by John Mitchum entitled **Why I Love Her** and I think it touches upon the feelings that hopefully anybody, anywhere can relate to their own country.

"America, America, God shed his grace on thee..."

You ask me Why I Love Her? Well, give me time and I'll explain.
Have you seen a Kansas sunset or an Arizona rain?
Have you drifted on a bayou down Louisiana way?
Have you watched a cold fog drifting over San Francisco Bay?

Have you heard a bobwhite calling in the Carolina pines,
Or heard the bellow of a diesel at the Appalachia mines?
Does the call of Niagara thrill you when you hear her waters roar?
Do you look with awe and wonder at her Massachusetts shore,

Where men who braved a hard new world first stepped on Plymouth's
rock?
And do you think of them when you stroll along a New York City
dock?

Have you seen a snowflake drifting in the Rockies way up high?
Have you seen the sun come blazing down from a bright Nevada sky?
Do you hail to the Columbia as she rushes to the sea,
Or bow your head at Gettysburg at our struggle to be free?

Have you seen the mighty Tetons? Have you watched an eagle soar?
Have you seen the Mississippi roll along Missouri's shore?
Have you felt a chill at Michigan when on a winter's day,
Her waters rage along the shore in thunderous display?
Does the word "Aloha" make you warm? Do you stare in disbelief,
When you see the surf come roaring in at Wiamea Reef.

From Alaska's cold to the Everglades, from the Rio Grand to Maine,
My heart cries out, my pulse runs fast at the might of her domain.
You ask me Why I Love Her? I've a million reasons why:
My beautiful America, beneath God's wide, wide sky.

"And crown thy good with brotherhood, from sea to shining sea."

FIGHT ONE MORE ROUND by James J. Corbett
When your feet are so tired that you have to shuffle back to the center
of the ring, fight one more round. When your arms are so tired that
you can hardly lift your hand to come on guard, fight one more round.
When your nose is bleeding and your eyes are black and you are so
tired that you wish your opponent would crack you one on the jaw
and put you to sleep, fight one more round - remembering that the
man who always fights one more round is never whipped.

145

Joys shared are doubled, sorrows shared are halved.
- Katherine Ferrari

Highway of Life
While we're speeding down the highway,
Let's count mileposts in sequence.
They all seem so close together,
Almost like a picket fence.
Our birthdays, too, are in the fast lane,
Which should make this thought serene:
From life's milestones to its tombstones,
There is little space between.
Hence, this moral: Let's start giving
Much less time to stress and strife;
While we race to make a living,
Let's take time TO MAKE A LIFE.   - Dave Wadley

"Do the thing, and you shall have the power; but they who do not do the thing have not the power." - Emerson

Here is something said by Abraham Lincoln that is worth thinking about: "Determine that the thing can and shall be done, and then we shall find the way."
In other words, before the way in which a thing can be done will clearly open up to us, two things must happen. And they must happen in us. First, we must be convinced that the thing can be done. It isn't enough simply to wish it could be done, or merely hope that we can be successful in it. We must know it can be done - and by us. Second, we must be determined that it will be done. And by us. We must have made the decision to do it.
Determine that you can and that you will, and you will find the way.

146

Now, follow through on that decision. From all your unfulfilled plans - choose one as your first objective. Now, select one definite step - one definite thing you can do toward that objective. Next, put that one step definitely on your schedule to be started at a specific time. When the time comes, let nothing stand in the way of starting it.
Do this and you'll have one of the most satisfying feelings inside that you've had in years. - Dr. Gene Emmet Clark

You only lose energy when life becomes dull in your mind. Your mind gets bored and therefore tired of doing nothing. Get interested in something! Get absolutely enthralled in something! Get out of yourself! Be somebody! Do something. The more you lose yourself in something bigger than yourself, the more energy you will have.
- Norman Vincent Peale

WAYS TO DISCOVER JOY
1. Celebrate Freedom
2. Expect the Best
3. Laugh a Lot
4. Take the Initiative
5. Express Admiration
6. Put Others First
7. Send Out Positive Energy
8. Inspire Someone

The key to achievement lies in being a HOW thinker, not an IF thinker.

There has been 11 billion people to walk this earth, but there has never been one like you. Ask yourself a question: Is my attitude worth catching?

Pay attention to those who speak with you, and you will tell them more than your words ever could.

Pay attention to those who love you, and the love will grow.

Pay attention to your garden, and it will be full of lush, bright color.

Pay attention to your work, and you'll achieve great things.

Pay attention to your community, and it will be a wonderful place to live.

Pay attention to the direction of your life, and you will find fulfillment.

One of the greatest things you have to give is your attention. Listen, watch, understand, respond. Just think of all the problems which are the result of people not paying attention - to their work, to their children, to their spouses, to where their life is headed, to the society in which they live.

Paying attention is not easy. There are so many distractions. Just like anything else worthwhile, paying attention takes effort and intention. And just like anything else worth doing, the rewards far outweigh the sacrifice. Pay attention, and it will pay you back.
- Author Unknown

If people like you they'll listen to you, but if they trust you they'll do business with you.

FOUR THINGS WILL NEVER RETURN:
The spoken word,
The sped arrow,
Time past,
The neglected opportunity.

Friends are a very rare jewel, indeed. They make you smile and encourage you to succeed. They lend an ear, they share a word of praise, and they always want to open their hearts to us. Show your friends how much you care.

Positive People Power

Wonderful
Words of
Wisdom

"Be like a postage stamp.
Stick to one thing
until you get there."
-Josh Billings

Only the Best

Often we become so wrapped up in our own business that we have blinded ourselves to the sacrifices others make for us, the kind of sacrifices that only those who love us would make:

There was a couple who had celebrated their golden anniversary with a big party. Presents were exchanged, and congratulations were expressed before they got in their car and drove home.

When they got home the woman made her way into the kitchen.

As was her custom, she brewed some tea, and took out a loaf of bread, one of which she had baked daily for years. She cut off the heel, warmed it, and buttered it for her husband before cutting another slice for herself. Then she served him the warm bread.

Now, this guy who had been married for fifty years loved his wife greatly, but the stress of the day had taken its toll. And he blew up. He said, "Honey I love you. You know that. But quite frankly this is it. For more years than I can even count, you have baked bread for me every day. But you always give me the heel. You always pass off that crusty piece of bread, that heel on me. I have had it! I won't take it anymore!"

And this is true - she looked at him, blinked back the tears and said, "But honey, that's my favorite piece."

Love is the language that is understood everywhere!

Don't Wait Till It's Too LATE

Thomas Carlyle learned too late the importance of sharing his life with the one who was closest to him while she was still able to experience it. I think we all need to be reminded of this from time to time during our busy schedules.

Thomas Carlyle lived from 1795 until 1881. He was a Scot essayist and historian. During his lifetime he became one of the world's greatest writers. But he was a human and humans make mistakes.

On October 17, 1826, Carlyle married his secretary Jane Welsh. She was an intelligent, attractive and somewhat temperamental daughter of a well-to-do doctor. They had their quarrels and misunderstandings, but still loved each other dearly. After their marriage, Jane continued to serve as his secretary. After many years of marriage, Jane became ill.

Being a hard worker, Carlyle became so absorbed in his writings that he let Jane continue working for several weeks after she became ill. She had cancer, and it was one of the slow growing kind. Finally, she became confined to her bed.

Although Carlyle loved her dearly, he very seldom found time to stay with her long. He was busy with his work. When Jane died they carried her to the cemetery for the service. The day was a miserable day. It was raining hard and the mud was deep.

Following the funeral Carlyle went back to his home. He was taking it pretty hard. He went up the stairs to Jane's room and sat down in the chair next to her bed. He sat there thinking about how little time he had spent with her and wishing so much he had a chance to do it differently.

Noticing her diary on a table beside the bed, he picked it up and began to read in it. Suddenly he seemed shocked. He saw it. There, on one page, she had written a single line. "Yesterday he spent an hour with me and it was like heaven; I love him so."

Something dawned on him that he had not noticed before. He had been too busy to notice that he meant so much to her. He thought of all the times he had gone about his work without thinking about and noticing her.

Then Carlyle turned the page in the diary. There he noticed written some words that broke his heart. "I have listened all day to hear his steps in the hall, but now it is late and I guess he won't come today." Carlyle read a little more in the book.

Then he threw it down and ran out of the house. Some of his friends found him at the grave, his face buried in the mud. His eyes were red from weeping. Tears continued to roll down his cheeks. He kept repeating over and over again, "If I had only known, if I had only known."
But it was too late for Carlyle. She was dead.

After Jane's death, Carlyle made little attempt to write again. The historian said he lived another 15 years, "Weary, bored and a partial recluse."

I tell the story with the hope that you will not make the same mistake. While our loved ones must have the money we make to live, it is the love we have that they really want. Give it now before it is too late.

You have brains in your head.
You have feet in your shoes.
You can steer yourself
any direction you choose.
You're on your own
And you know what you know,
And YOU are the guy
Who'll decide where to go.
- Oh, the Places You'll Go - Dr. Seuss

Positive thinking will let you do everything better than negative thinking will.

One man owned a small estate and wished to sell it. He sent for an agent and asked him to write an advertisement telling about the estate. When the ad was ready, the agent took it to the gentleman and read it to him.
"Read that again," said the owner. The agent read the description once more.
"I don't think I'll sell after all," said the man. "I've been looking for an estate like this all my life, and I didn't know that I owned it."
Have you ever felt that way? Dissatisfied until you took inventory of yourself? It's not hard to count up our liabilities. **But have you assessed your assets?????**- Steve Goodier

You never know how far you can reach until you stretch.

Sales Tip from Brian Tracy
Here is a simply exercise you can perform called the "3-3-3 analysis."
This analysis consists of three answers to each of three questions.
1. List three reasons why someone should purchase your product or service at all, from your company or from some other company;
2. List three reasons why someone who has decided to buy your product or service should buy it from your company rather than from some other company;
3. List three reasons why a prospect should buy your product or service from you personally rather than from some other salesperson in your company.

Efficiency is doing things right. Effectiveness is doing the right things efficiently.

The way you get out of a job you don't like is to do it so extraordinarily well that nobody can afford to keep you in that position.

When you learn how to set one goal, you'll know how to set all goals. A task worth doing...and friends worth having...make life worth living.

* STEPS TO HAPPINESS
Everybody Knows:
You can't be all things to all people.
You can't do all things at once.
You can't do all things equally well.
You can't do all things better than everyone else.
Your humanity is showing just like everyone else's.
So:

You have to find out who you are, and be that.
You have to decide what comes first, and do that.
You have to discover your strengths, and use them.
You have to learn not to compete with others,
Because no one else is in the contest of "being you".
Then:
You will have learned to accept your own uniqueness.
You will have learned to set priorities and make decisions.
You will have learned to live with your limitations.
You will have learned to give yourself the respect that is due.
And you'll be a most vital mortal.
Dare To Believe:
That you are a wonderful, unique person.
That you are a once-in-all-history event.
That it's more than a right, it's your duty, to be who you are.
That life is not a problem to solve, but a gift to cherish.
And you'll be able to stay one up on what used to get you down

Love is the ingredient that makes every relationship in life, whatever it is, a little better. Love has a capacity to mend the broken, heal the hurting, and inspire the despairing. Love that reaches beyond the misunderstandings and the failures is a love that unites and encourages. Such a love is one of our world's greatest needs.
 - C. Neil Strait

I expect to pass through this world but once. Any good therefore that I can do, or any kindness that I can show to any fellow creature let me do it now. Let me not defer or neglect it, for I shall not pass this way again. - Stephen Grellet

He slept beneath the moon,
He basked beneath the sun,
He lived a life of going to do,
And died with nothing done.
- From James Albery, 1838-1899 epitaph said to be written by himself.

A friend is one who walks in when the rest of the world walks out.

Write on your heart that everyday is the best day of the year.
  - Emerson

Our company requires no further physical fitness programs. Everyone get enough exercise jumping to conclusions, flying off the handle, beating around the bush, running down the boss, going around in circles, dragging their feet, dodging responsibility, passing the buck, climbing the ladder, wadding through paperwork, pulling strings, throwing their weight around, stretching the truth, bending the rules and pushing their luck. - Joseph Ruffo

How most people spend their valuable time!
Americans spend:
-five years of their life standing in line.
-two years trying to return phone calls.
-eight months opening direct mail.
-six years eating.
-one year searching for misplaced objects.
-and four years on major household chores.

The following poem, to me, represents taking a chance. You don't know for sure the results of what you may be risking, but the rewards may be great. It's like throwing a stone into the water and watching the ripples go out in all directions. Take a chance and throw out some positive action today and watch the ripple effect.

The Arrow and the Song
I shot an arrow into the air,
It fell to earth, I knew not where;
For, so swiftly it flew, the sight
Could not follow it in its flight.

I breathed a song into the air,
It fell to earth, I knew not where;
For who has sight so keen and strong
That it can follow the flight of song?

Long, long afterward, in an oak
I found the arrow, still unbroken;
And the song, from beginning to end,
I found again in the heart of a friend.
- Henry Wadsworth Longfellow

HOW TO BE MORE PERSUASIVE
All of us need to be more persuasive if we want to get more accomplished when serving our clients, proposing new items, dealing with employees, and all the many other jobs confronting us.
Here is a list of the twelve most persuasive words, chosen by researchers at Yale University. They are: You, health, easy, guarantee, love, money, discovery, new, proven, save, results, and safety.

We cannot control the tragic things that happen to us, but we can control the way we face up to them.

Hard work and ambition can carry you far, even if you don't have much formal education. A junk dealer in a northeastern state who became a millionaire never got beyond the eighth grade. When asked how he managed to do so well in spite of his handicaps, the fellow replied: "Well, it ain't hard really. I just buy things for a $1 and sell them for four $4. You'd be surprised how fast that 3% profit piles up."

Any time we're tempted to think that our technology has gone about as far as it can go, we should stop and remember a certain Commissioner of the U.S. Patent Office. In 1895, he proposed to Congress that the Patent Office be closed, because all the great inventions had already been made.

Difficulties are meant to rouse, not discourage. - William Channing

Michael is the kind of guy you love to hate. He is always in a good mood and always has something positive to say. When someone would ask him how he was doing, he would reply, "If I were any better, I would be twins!"
He was a natural motivator. If an employee was having a bad day, Michael was there telling the employee how to look on the positive side of the situation. Seeing this style really made me curious, so one, day I went up to Michael and asked him, "I don't get it! You can't be a positive person all of the time. How do you do it?"
Michael replied, "Each morning I wake up and say to myself, Mike, you have two choices today. You can choose to be in a good mood or you can choose to be in a bad mood. "I choose to be in a good mood. Each time something bad happens, I can choose to be a victim or I can choose to learn from it. I choose to learn from it. Every time someone comes to me complaining, I can choose to accept their

complaining or I can point out the positive side of life. I choose the positive side of life."

"Yeah, right, it isn't that easy," I protested. "Yes, it is," Michael said. "Life is all about choices. When you cut away all the junk, every situation is a choice. You choose how you react to situations. You choose how people will affect your mood. You choose to be in a good mood or bad mood. The bottom line is: It's your choice how you live life."

I reflected on what Michael said. Soon thereafter, I left the Tower Industry to start my own business. We lost touch, but I often thought about him when I made a choice about life instead of reacting to it.

Several years later, I heard that Michael was involved in a serious accident, falling some 60 feet from a communications tower. After 18 hours of surgery and weeks of intensive care, Michael was released from the hospital with rods placed in his back. I saw Michael about six months after the accident.

When I asked him how he was, he replied. "If I were any better, I would be twins. Wanna see my scars?" I declined to see his wounds, but did ask him what had gone through his mind as the accident took place.

"The first thing that went through my mind was the well being of my soon to be born daughter," Michael replied. "Then, as I lay on the ground, I remembered that I had two choices: I could choose to live or I could choose to die. "I chose to live."

"Weren't you scared? Did you lose consciousness?" I asked. Michael continued, "...the paramedics were great. They kept telling me I was going to be fine. But when they wheeled me into the ER and I saw the expressions on the faces of the doctors and nurses, I got really scared. In their eyes, I read "he's a dead man. I knew I needed to take action."

"What did you do?" I asked.

"Well, there was a big burly nurse shouting questions at me," said Michael. "She asked if I was allergic to anything. 'Yes', I replied. The doctors and nurses stopped working as they waited for my reply. I took a deep breath and yelled, "Gravity." Over their laughter, I told them, 'I am choosing to live. Operate on me as if I am alive, not dead'."

Michael lived, thanks to the skill of his doctors, but also because of his amazing attitude. I learned from him that every day we have the choice to live fully. Attitude, after all, is everything.

You have two choices now:

1. Forget this.

2. Pass it on to the people you care about.

I hope you will choose #2. I did.

I like the dreams of the future better than the history of the past.

- Thomas Jefferson

A Mother's Memories...

The baby is teething. The children are fighting. Your husband just called, "Eat dinner without me."

One of these days, you'll explode and shout to the kids, "Why don't you grow up?" And they will.

You'll straighten their bedrooms all neat and tidy, toys displayed on the shelf, hangers in the closet, animals caged. You'll say, "Now I want it to stay this way." And it will.

You will prepare a perfect dinner with a salad that hasn't had all the olives picked out and a cake with no finger traces in the icing and you'll say, "Now this is a meal for company." And you will eat it alone.

You'll yell, "I want complete privacy on the phone. No screaming. Do you hear me?" And no one will answer.

No more plastic tablecloths stained with spaghetti. No more dandelion bouquets. No more iron-on patches. No more wet, knotted shoelaces, muddy boots, or rubber bands for ponytails...
No more Christmas presents made of library paste and toothpicks. No wet oatmeal kisses. No more tooth fairy. No more giggles in the dark...scraped knees to kiss or sticky fingers to clean. Only a voice asking, "Why don't you grow up?"
And the silence echoes: "I did."- Author Unknown

Life is lived in the present. Yesterday has gone, tomorrow is yet to be. Today is the miracle.

Jim,
Following is an assignment a student turned in for a "Creative Appreciation" exercise. I thought you might enjoy it.   -Dean
Person Chosen: Mother
Gift Chosen to Give: Stethoscope Award:
"Thanks for always listening close to my heart"
"My mother has always been my best friend and I do not get to thank her enough for listening and always being there for me. I gave her a stethoscope as the gift and included a card that read, "Thanks for always listening close to my heart." My mother lives in Louisiana so I had to mail it to her. I actually overnighted it to her because it was very important. She called and was extremely touched."

The best way to destroy an enemy is to make him your friend.

Luck is seldom the fickle lady she is often pictured as being. She is more apt to bestow her favors on the deserving than the undeserving. She is especially apt to smile on people who work hard.
Alexander Graham Bell's wife was practically deaf, and for months he worked passionately to invent a workable hearing aid for her. Just

163

as it seemed he had failed, his work led to the discovery of the principles for the telephone.

Luck had smiled -- but Bell deserved it.

Find yourself and be yourself: remember there is no one else on earth like you. - Dale Carnegie

Laugh a little - sing a little
As you go your way!
Work a little - play a little,
Do this every day!
Give a little - take a little,
Never mind a frown -
Make your smile a welcomed thing
All around the town!
Laugh a little - love a little,
Skies are always blue!
Every cloud has silver linings,
But it's up to you.

Real leaders see vast possibilities and sell their dreams to their companies, their employees, their funding sources, their government and their buying public.

What distinguishes a great leader from a good leader? Here are the characteristics of great leaders, according to Small Business reports:

Courage - Great leaders have the courage to make decisions and stand behind them.

Willpower - Great leaders are determined to carry through decisions in spite of opposition.

Judgment - Great leaders can balance the pros and cons of any situation.

Flexibility - Great leaders adapt successfully to change.
Knowledge - Great leaders yearn to learn.
Integrity - Great leaders are committed to honesty and guided by a business sense built on values people admire and respect.

Leaders know that working on themselves is a full-time job. The more and better their self-work, the better work they can get from those they employ and less fault and complaints they have with those around them.   - Mark Victor Hansen

<u>A Winner's Touch</u>
I am a winner!
I have a powerful, winning feeling.
I act like a winner.
I consistently handle my life and all my responsibilities in a winning manner.
I put forth a winning effort in all I do.
I take charge of my day by consciously choosing to feel like a winner.
I am a winner!
I have a winner's touch.
I think like a winner.
I walk like a winner.
I talk like a winner.
I perform like a winner.
I receive the applause of a winner.
I accept the rewards that come to a winner.
Why?
Because I am a winner!   - Jack Boland

How to Tell a Winner from a Loser
A winner says, "let's find out,
A loser says, "Nobody knows."
When a winner makes a mistake, he says, "I was wrong."
When a loser makes a mistake, he says, "It wasn't my fault."
A winner goes through a problem.
A loser goes around it, and never gets past it.
A winner says, "I'm good, but not as good as I ought to be."
A loser says, "I'm not as bad as a lot of other people."
A winner tries to learn from those superior to him.
A loser tries to tear down those who are superior to him.
A winner says, "There ought to be a better way to do it."
A loser says, "That's the way it's always been done here."
Let's hear it for the winners!!!

Thoughts of a Winner
Although I am only one out of a million, I am somebody and that
makes me as good as the next person.
There is nothing in this life I cannot do. There is no goal I cannot
tackle and, have success. If I feel deep down inside that something
is important to me, then I can do it. If my mind can conceive it and
believe it, then I know I can achieve it. No longer will I drift through
life feeling sorry for myself, because self-pity is the seed of
destruction.
I will search for a goal, and with enough hard work, total
commitment, determination, dedication, and self-sacrifice, I know I
will reach it. I know there will be many times when it will seem that
all the odds are against me, and I will have to fight one battle after
another - but I will not give up. - Author Unknown

166

Putting it all in perspective...

In 1555, Ivan the Terrible ordered the construction of St. Basil's Cathedral in Moscow. He was so thrilled with the work done by the two architects that he had them blinded so they could never be able to build anything else more beautiful.

All of a sudden, that small raise you got last week doesn't seem so bad, does it?

Nothing in life is more exciting and rewarding than the sudden flash of insight that leaves you a changed person - not only changed, but for the better.   - Arthur Gordon

One Sunday morning, I went to the grocery store to get some milk for breakfast. As I paid for he milk, the clerk asked me if I needed a bag for the milk. I said, "No." Then she said, "Well, I need a smile!"

That incident made me think on the value of a smile and how it affects our attitude and others. A smile on your face the first thing in the morning can help to make your day more alive and exciting. So that made me think, when you look in the mirror in the mornings, what do you see?

Do you see a bright, alert, smiling, enthusiastic, excited, happy, motivated person, who is anxiously looking forward to the start of another day full of opportunities?

.........or...............

Do you see a dull, glazed, stressed-out, frowning, grouchy, defeated person, who hates the ideas that he has to go to work because he knows this is going to be another one of those awful days.

Well, the fact is, that when you look in the mirror...

What you see, IS what you get! So if you want your day to be the best that it can be, then SMILE at yourself and tell yourself that you are going to have one of the most SUPER TERRIFIC days of your life.

167

If you do this with the attitude that this is going to come true, you will find that it will come true. It's the self-fulfilling prophesy. What we wish to happen, usually happens. Unfortunately, we usually think the worst and the worst is what happens. So, look in the mirror and see the person you would like to have as your best friend and then act the part. You will get what you see!

YESTERDAY - could be a magic word. How many times have you said, "Well, yesterday, I could have done that for you", or "Yesterday, I knew this was going to happen".

Yesterday has a magic about it that is hard to explain. It could be we only remember the good things that happened so yesterday is always filled with good memories. And Yesterday can also be more than one day in our lives. Why it seems like only yesterday, that the children were just starting school. Or I remember it like it was only yesterday. Yesterday gives us the chance to put things in proper order, even if it didn't occur that way. Yesterday was not quite like I wanted it to be so when I recount the activities I tell it the way I would have liked for it to happen. I do not lie, I just reorganize.

But, it doesn't matter what I remember from yesterday, because you will remember it differently and so will Joe and Mary and Bob and Ruth and Frank and Jane and Biff and Buffy. Everybody has a different recollection of the way things were in that brief moment of time which was and is yesterday.

Just like the Beatles song, "Yesterday, all my troubles seem so far away, now I need a place to hide away, cause I believe in yesterday". Today is the tomorrow you dreamed about yesterday.

Thanks to Susan Arnold for The Second Ten Commandments.
1. Thou shall not worry,
    for worry is the most unproductive of all human activities.
2. Thou shall not be fearful,

for most of the things we fear never come to pass.

3. Thou shall not cross bridges before you come to them,
   for no one yet has succeeded in accomplishing this.

4. Thou shall face each problem as it comes.
   You can only handle one at a time anyway.

5. Thou shall not take problems to bed with you,
   for they make very poor bedfellows.

6. Thou shall not borrow other people's problems.
   They can better care for them than you can.

7. Thou shall not try to relive yesterday for good or ill,
   it is forever gone. Concentrate on what is happening
   in your life and be happy now!

8. Thou shall be a good listener,
   for only when you listen do you hear ideas different from
   your own. It is hard to learn something new when you are
   talking, and some people do know more than you do.

9. Thou shall not become "bogged down" by frustration,
   for 90% of it is rooted in self-pity and will only
   interfere with positive action.

10. Thou shall count thy blessings,
    never overlooking the small ones,
    for a lot of small blessings add up to a big one. -Author Unknown

If your cup runneth over, expand your cup. When you accomplish a goal, never cross it out. Just write "victory" next to it and move on to the next one. That way, whenever you have a mediocre day, review your victories and you'll say, "atta boy" or "atta girl" to yourself. - Mark Victor Hansen

Having clear objectives in life is very important. Because in the absence of a goal to be achieved, you have no standard for judging whether you are getting anywhere. Simply, your life can't go according to plan if you have no plan. Goals are important because they give you a feeling of purpose. Goals are something you can aim your life toward. They are a destination -- something to reach for. They give you direction. The challenges involved in reaching a goal bring growth and develop character. When you accomplish your goals you experience the joy of achievement.

One of the major causes of failing to reach a goal is that many people get so concerned about the possible obstacles they are likely to encounter that they give up before they ever start. Begin today and define what it is you want from life. It is essential to know exactly and specifically what you want. Write your desires down on paper. Don't worry about how far the target is. Just keep sight of the bull's eye. Then take aim with desire, focus, and persistence and fire away!

The law of culture is to let each of us become all that we are capable of being.

GO FOR THE GOAL

Fortunate are the persons,
Who in this life can find
A purpose that can fill their days,
And goals to fill their minds!

The world is filled with many people,
Content with where they are;
Not knowing joys success can bring,
No will to go that far.

Yet in this world there is a need
For people to lead the rest,
To rise above the "average" life,
By giving of their best!

Would you be the one who dares to try
When challenged by the task?
To rise to heights you've never seen,
Or is that too much to ask?

This is your day -- a world to win,
Great purpose to achieve
Accept the challenge of your goals
And in yourself believe!

Life is like riding a bicycle. You don't fall off unless you stop pedaling.

There is an infinite distance between the wishers and the doers. A mere desire is lukewarm water, which will never take a train to its destination; the purpose must boil, must be made into live steam to do the work. Who would have ever heard of Theodore Roosevelt outside of his immediate community if he had only half committed himself to what he had undertaken, if he had brought only a part of himself to his task? The great secret of his career has been that he has flung his whole life, not a part of it, with all the determination and energy and power he could muster, into everything he has undertaken. No dillydallying, no faint-hearted efforts, no lukewarm purpose for him! - Orison Sweet Marden

There is not a shortcut. Victory lies in overcoming obstacles every day.

Character is the foundation stone upon which one must build to win respect. Just as no worthy building can be erected on a weak foundation, so no lasting reputation worthy of respect can be built on

171

a weak character. Without character, all effort to attain dignity is superficial, and the results are sure to be disappointing.
 - R.C. Samsel

Character is like the foundation of a house; it can be found below the surface. People of strong character will always do what they say they will do, when they say they will do it. They are dependable and truthful when it comes to keeping a commitment.

We are all builders of a sort. Some build houses, computers, cars, products of every sort, but one thing we all build whether we are aware of it or not is character. Laying the foundation of good character means never taking ethical shortcuts, but doing the right thing because it's the right thing to do. You can never maintain the integrity of your character through deceit and dishonesty. The true test of a person's character is in what they would do if they knew that no one would ever know.

If I could do whatever I wanted, without consequences of being seen by others, what would I be like and what would I do? Would I:
-shoplift items from a store?
-cheat on an exam?
-illegally copy computer software?
-invade someone's privacy to spy on him/her?
-steal from my employer?
-cheat on my tax return?
Or would I possess the virtues, such as honesty, respect, and self-discipline necessary to refrain from these actions?

Every day what you think, say, and do will add to or subtract from your character. Develop honesty, truthfulness, respect and dependability within yourself and you will never have to worry about your reputation nor jeopardize your character.

Your character is your destiny. Character is the ethical sense of what you are in your essence, the sum total of your habits, your personal assortment of virtues and vices.

Destiny is not a matter of chance, it is a matter of choice.
- William Jennings Bryan

From the diary of Anne Frank: "I have one outstanding trait in my character which must strike anyone who knows me for any length of time, and that is my knowledge of myself. I can watch myself and my actions, just like an outsider. The Anne of everyday I can face entirely without prejudice, without making excuses for her, and watch what's good and what's bad about her. This "self-consciousness" haunts me, and every time I open my mouth I know as soon as I've spoken whether "that ought to have been different" or "that was right as it was." There are so many things about myself that I condemn; I couldn't begin to name them all. I understand more and more how true Daddy's words were when he said: "All children must look after their own upbringing." Parents can only give good advice or put them on the right paths, but the final forming of a person's character lies in their own hands."
Three weeks after Anne wrote this passage, she and her family was arrested and sent to concentration camps and seven months later Anne died of typhus.
Anne's passage makes the point: You and you alone, ultimately determine your final character. As an adult, the responsibility for becoming a good person is ultimately yours and nobody else's. Not his, not hers, not theirs --just yours!

What you are will show in what you do. - Thomas A. Edison

When you judge another, you do not define them, you define yourself. - Wayne Dyer

When you're through changing, you're through. Be more concerned with your character than your reputation, because your character is what you really are, while your reputation is merely what others think you are. - John Wooden

The most important thing you can do to achieve your goals is to make sure that as soon as you set them, you immediately begin to create momentum. The most important rules that I ever adopted to help me in achieving my goals were those I learned from a very successful man who taught me to first write down the goal, and then to never leave the site of setting a goal without first taking some form of positive action toward its attainment. - Anthony Robbins

How to get the competitive edge - Read, every day, something no one else is reading. Think, every day, something no one else is thinking. Do, every day, something no one else would be silly enough to do. It is bad for the mind to be always part of unanimity.
- Christopher Morley

21 Action Steps for a 21st Century Leader - Denis Waitley
* Act self employed, but be a team player
* Be flexible in the face of daily surprises
* Take a proactive approach to your health
* Conduct a personal inventory of your knowledge resources
* Increase your reading, writing, and vocabulary proficiency
* Constantly upgrade your computer literacy

* Become a global network
* Create your personal presence on the World Wide Web
* Be responsible for your own financial security
* Start living in prime time
* Balance your time at work with many vacations
* Model yourself after the best individuals
* Set up a learning resource at home
* Be a person who practices non-situational integrity
* Attend the most important meetings you will ever have (with yourself)
* Balance high-tech with a high-touch environment
* Institute a more dynamic, proactive system for getting back to people
* Repeat business and profitability are directly related to relationships of trust
* Keep your personal and professional life in balance
* Create your own mission statement for your personal and professional life
* Chase your passion, not your pension

This coming week, take time to: fall asleep counting your blessings, embrace chaos, keep meetings short and productive, reinvent the wheel, imagine the most pleasurable fill-in-the-blank, and get to know your neighbors.

* Just wanted to let you know that I really like your positive thoughts for the day. I make time to read them. I saw something at camp 20 years ago that says a lot in a small way. - Thought it might make a good positive thought for someone else.
"Life is a Mystery to be Lived - Not a Problem to be Solved"
Take care, Robin

I'd like to share with you this story I came across in a Guidepost magazine in about 1970. It's about saying, Thank You!

We were a group of friends in the midst of an after-dinner conversation. Because Thanksgiving was just around the corner and prosperity wasn't, we fell to talking about what we had to be thankful for.

One of us said, "Well I, for one, am grateful to Mrs. Wendt, an old school teacher who, 30 years ago in a little West Virginia town, went out of her way to introduce me to the works of the poet, Tennyson." Then he launched into a colorful description of Mrs. Wendt, a lovely little old lady who had been his high school teacher and who evidently had made a deep impression on his life. She had gone out of her way to awaken his literary interest and develop his gifts of expression.

"And does this Mrs. Wendt know that she made that contribution to your life?" someone put in.

"I'm afraid she doesn't. I have been careless and have never, in all these years, told her either face-to-face or by letter."

"Then why don't you write her? It would make her happy if she is still living, and it might make you happier, too. The thing that most of us ought to do is to learn to develop the attitude of gratitude.

Now, all this is very poignant to me, because Mrs. Wendt was my teacher and I was the fellow who hadn't written. That friend's challenge made me see that I had accepted something very precious and hadn't bothered to say thanks.

That very evening, I tried to atone. On the chance that Mrs. Wendt, might still be living, I sat down and wrote her what I call a Thanksgiving letter. I reminded her that it was she who had introduced my young mind to the works of Tennyson and Browning and others.

It took a couple of weeks for the Post Office to search for Mrs. Wendt with my letter. It was forwarded from town to town. Finally it reached her, and this is the handwritten note I had in return. It began: *"My Dear Willie,"*
The introduction itself was quite enough to warm my heart. Here I was, a man of 50, fat and bald, addressed as "Willie." I had to smile over that, and then I read on:

"I remember well your enthusiasm for Tennyson and the Idylls of the Kings when I read them to you, for you were so beautifully responsive. My reward for telling you about Tennyson did not have to wait until your belated note of thanks came to me in my old age. I received my best reward in your eager response to the lyrical beauty and the idealism of Tennyson.

But, in spite of the fact that I got much of my reward at that time, I want you to know what your note meant to me. I am now an old lady in my 80's, living alone in a small room, cooking my own meals, lonely and seemingly like the last leaf of fall left behind.

You will be interested to know, Willie, that I taught school for 50 years and, in all that time, yours is the first note of appreciation I ever received. It came on a blue, cold morning, and it cheered my lonely old heart as nothing has cheered me in many years."

I wept over that simple, sincere note from my teacher of long ago. I read it to a dozen friends. One of them said, "I believe I'm going to write Miss Mary Scott a letter. She did something similar to that for my boyhood."

That first Thanksgiving letter was so successful and satisfying that I made a list of people who had contributed something definite and lasting to my life and planned to write at least one Thanksgiving letter every day in November.

For 10 years, I have kept up this exciting game of writing Thanksgiving month letters. I have a special file for answers, and now I have more than 500 of the most beautiful letters anyone has ever received.

One of the most beautiful and touching letters came from the late Bishop William F. McDowell, in whose Washington home I had found some needed rest before a speaking engagement. Seeing that I was tired, Mrs. McDowell put me to bed to rest and I was so grateful for that motherly thoughtfulness that I never forgot. And yet, I had never written her a letter of thanks.

When I started in on my Thanksgiving letters I remembered her and, knowing that she was gone, I wrote my thank-you letter to the Bishop, going over the memory and telling him all about it. I received this:

My Dear Will,
"Your Thanksgiving letter, as you called it, was so beautiful, so real, that as I sat reading it in my study the tears fell from eyes, tears of gratitude. Then, before I realized what I was doing, I arose from my chair, called her name and started to show it to her - for the moment forgetting she was gone. You will never know how much your letter has warmed my spirit. I have been walking about in the glow of it all day long."

A Thanksgiving letter isn't much. Only a few lines are necessary, and a stamp to mail it. But the rewards are so great that eternity alone can estimate them. Thanks to the rebuke of a friend, I have learned a little, at least, about gratitude. -Written by William L. Stidger

I have been writing letters for almost 30 years now and have received many wonderful letters in return. One from my dear friend, the late Dick Semann said:

Jim, Thanks so much for your "Thanksgiving Letter." I can't tell you how much it meant to me...and...it came at a time when I needed a boost! Bless you...

Recently I wrote a letter to a friend to tell him how much he had meant to me over the years...and he told me later that he wept when he received it...I now know how he felt...When I got the letter at the post office I began to read it on the way home, (not the safest thing to do!) When I finished, I had to stop the car - I couldn't see the road for the tears in my eyes...Thanks so much for making my day...and ...giving me a great "THANKSGIVING"...
Sincerely, Dick
This may be a tradition you would like to start in your life. I hope so!

Confidence is the inner voice that says you are becoming what you are capable of being.

Seek not outside yourself, success is within. - Mary Lou Cook

Tools
For
Success

**"It is not the strongest
of the species that survive,
nor the most intelligent,
but the one
most responsive to change.
- Charles Darwin**

TOOLS FOR SUCCESS-

THE POSITIVE POWERED GOAL POSTER is the process of creating a concrete visual picture of yourself - being, enjoying, doing, and achieving the things you truly desire. This is accomplished by gathering articles, pictures, symbols, photos, words, and making a poster. The resulting POSITIVE POWERED GOAL POSTER shows you living, having and experiencing your goal in the present tense. It will become a lasting visual image of you achieving success which you will turn to often to inspire and reinforce your mind to clearly focus on your lifetime goals and dreams.

HOW CAN A POSITIVE POWERED GOAL POSTER HELP YOU?

There is a little known secret of success found in the power of visualization and the POSITIVE POWERED GOAL POSTER is one of the most powerful methods of visualization known to man. Visualization means to form a picture of something in your mind which is not in sight. It is important to know that human beings think through pictures - not through thoughts, words or feelings - but through pictures in the mind. We think words, which creates pictures in our mind, which causes us to have feelings about the thought. The POSITIVE POWERED GOAL POSTER takes advantage of the awesome power of visualization. To prove how strong is the connection between words, pictures and feelings, try the following test. **DON'T THINK OF A PENGUIN!** It is almost impossible for anyone not to have a picture of a penguin flash into their mind. When someone says don't, most of us do. That's why we should always phrase our conversations in the affirmative. You tell someone not to step into mud puddle and the picture of them stepping into the mud puddle appears in the mind's eye and they step into the mud puddle.

So anytime you try to think of something without a picture flashing through your mind, you will find it almost impossible. Anything we do - whether it's driving a car, skiing downhill or winning the lottery - starts with a mental picture. If you reflect on your life, you will see this is true. By keeping a clear picture in your mind of <u>your goal</u>, you can <u>achieve anything</u> you desire.

You can break through your barriers of success by creating positive new beliefs. Every picture tells a story; and it's true - a picture is worth a thousand words. You can use photo illustrations - whether you take them yourself or cut them from magazines - to create powerful self-image pictures that have a dramatic impact on your ability to imprint your mind with positive new beliefs about the future possibilities you're designing for yourself.

For example, if there's a particular car you want, take a camera to the dealer, select the make, model and color of the car of your choice, and have the salesperson take a few shots of you in the driver's seat and paste these pictures in your book.

THREE BELIEFS NECESSARY TO INFLUENCE YOUR POSITIVE POWERED GOAL POSTER!

1. What you see is what you get -

People who are successful always believe they will get what they want. They have the confidence in their abilities and visualize themselves having what they want before they go after it. If you do not have the positive belief that you can truly have what you want, then you can expect to experience all kinds of problems, missed opportunities, limitations and "this always happens to me." You can change your belief in what is possible for you. Your life is not set in concrete, it is flexible and can be changed by changing your thoughts. Positive thoughts, words and pictures create positive results.

2. What you want, you can have -

There is unlimited abundance in the universe and anything you want can be yours by activating your positive thoughts and visualizations. You are entitled to anything you want as long as it harms no one else. You can really get whatever you want if you go about the proper way of getting it.

3. What you want, you deserve -

You deserve and are entitled to whatever you desire. There is nothing you cannot have, if you believe. You must now see yourself as the most deserving person in the world. You must see yourself as a positive, caring, sharing, wonderful, successful person and because of this, you deserve the best.

With these beliefs, fully imbedded in your brain, you are now ready to formulate your POSITIVE POWERED GOAL POSTER!

WHAT DO I NEED TO MAKE MY GAME PLAN POSITIVE POWERED GOAL POSTER?

One, you need or have the desire to achieve your goal and two, you need or have the commitment to plan your way to success in that goal. Three, you need time to plan, construct and reflect upon your POSITIVE POWERED GOAL POSTER in a positive, meaningful manner.

Finally, you need the materials necessary to make your POSITIVE POWERED GOAL POSTER a reality.

* Poster board or paper, wood, fiberboard, cork board, etc.
* books, magazines, newspapers (used bookstores/thrifts or second-hand shops are a good place to find magazines)
* Glue, paste, scotch tape, thumbtacks, etc.
* Scissors
* pens, pencils, markers, stick-ons

* Photographs of yourself - (good source for quick photos are the photo machines which provide three or four photos inexpensively)

MAKING THE POSITIVE POWERED GOAL POSTER!

Calmly flip through your material looking for pictures, photos, advertisements and/or headlines that represent your vision of your goal.

EXAMPLE: If you want a trip to Hawaii you might select pictures or scenes of beaches, palm trees, surfers, sugar, pineapples, a couple walking on the beach, a tropical sunset, people on a ship or boat, activities such as fishing, swimming, strolling, eating, shopping, etc. Your goal of a trip to Hawaii may mean more to you, such as a place to reflect, meditate, a place of healing, discovery or a new adventure. Find pictures and any other items which will represent these experiences to you.

Cut out the pictures, assemble your items and arrange them on your poster board or any other surface you have selected for your POSITIVE POWERED GOAL POSTER. Evaluate your selections to make sure you have a complete visual picture of your goal. You can also make your own drawings or combine them with pictures. Add, subtract or rearrange your materials so that the resulting image is complete and aesthetically pleasing. Paste or otherwise secure them onto the surface. Don't forget to place photos of yourself anywhere you would like on the POSITIVE POWERED GOAL POSTER. Wherever there is a face of someone in a picture that might represent you, paste your face over it. If God is an important part of your life, add a symbol of your faith to the POSITIVE POWERED GOAL POSTER, such as a picture of Jesus or any personal religious image.

Your affirmations should also be added to the POSITIVE POWERED GOAL POSTER. For example, if your goal is to be a better student, your affirmation might be: "I enjoy studying and

184

working to improve my grades." You can also take crayons or markers and write key words in large letters such as; FUN, ADVENTURE, SUCCESS, LOVE, HEALTH, MONEY, which fit into the theme of your goal.

For greater results, use lots of color on your POSITIVE POWERED GOAL POSTER. Be creative and use your imagination. Add anything to your poster that will help you visualize your achievement of your goal. Have fun!

HOW TO USE YOUR POSITIVE POWERED GOAL POSTER

Using your POSITIVE POWERED GOAL POSTER is easy and requires very little time - yet the effort you put into working with it will bring dramatic results.

Review your poster or posters daily. Pick times that best fit your schedule, either in the morning before your day begins or in the evening before you go to sleep - preferably both.

As you look at the pictures and read the words, feel that you are this person "now" and that everything on the poster has already come into your life. Feel that the poster is an accomplished fact, even if it isn't so yet. Remember, your creative imagination cannot tell the difference between what is real and what you are imaging. To have the POSITIVE POWERED GOAL POSTER become "you" and part of your life, it needs to be a present tense experience - not a future one. Feel it now.

Your poster will act as an affirmation in visible form and as goals firmly set in mind. Focusing your attention on them daily will cause the law of mind action to work for you. That is, whatever you conceive of and believe in, you will achieve. This is accomplished by joining your conceptions with feelings of excitement, gratitude and a sense of already having accomplished these things you are rehearsing in your mind.

185

Knowing that you are taking action to achieve your inner and outer goals makes your life very exciting and fulfilling. Use the POSITIVE POWERED GOAL POSTER regularly and expect results.

Things do not happen. Things are made to happen.- John F. Kennedy

Dreams are the touchstones of our character. - Thoreau

You can become blind by seeing each day as a similar one. Each day is a different one, each day brings a miracle of its own. It's just a matter of paying attention to this miracle. -Paulo Coelho

Thanks to Grains of Sand for the following story.
I am a mother of three (ages 14, 12, 3) and have recently completed my college degree. The last class I had to take was Sociology. The teacher was absolutely inspiring with the qualities that I wish every human being had been graced with. Her last project of the term was called "Smile." The class was asked to go out and smile at three people and document their reactions. I am a very friendly person and always smile at everyone and say hello anyway.....so, I thought, this would be a piece of cake, literally.
Soon after we were assigned the project, my husband, youngest son, and I went out to McDonald's, one crisp March morning. It was just our way of sharing special play time with our son. We were standing in line, waiting to be served, when all of a sudden everyone around us began to back away, and then even my husband did. I did not move an inch...an overwhelming feeling of panic welled up inside of me as I turned to see why they had moved. As I turned around I smelled a horrible "dirty body" smell...and there standing behind me were two poor homeless men. As I looked down at the short gentleman, close to me, he was "smiling".

186

His beautiful sky blue eyes were full of God's Light as he searched for acceptance. He said, "Good day" as he counted the few coins he had been clutching. The second man fumbled with his hands as he stood behind his friend. I realized the second man was mentally deficient and the blue eyed gentleman was his salvation. I held my tears....as I stood there with them. The young lady at the counter asked him what they wanted.

He said, "Coffee is all, Miss" because that was all they could afford to sit in the restaurant and warm up, (they had to buy something...he just wanted to be warm). Then I really felt it... the compulsion was so great I almost reached out and embraced the little man with the blue eyes. That is when I noticed all eyes in the restaurant were set on me...judging my every action. I smiled and asked the young lady behind the counter to give me two more breakfast meals on a separate tray. I then walked around the corner to the table that the men had chosen as a resting spot. I put the tray on the table and laid my hand on the blue eyed gentleman's cold hand. He looked up at me, with tears in his eyes, and said, "Thank you."

I leaned over, began to pat his hand and said, "I did not do this for you...God is here working through me to give you hope." I started to cry as I walked away to join my husband and son. When I sat down my husband smiled at me and said, "That is why God gave you to me, Honey....to give me hope."

We held hands for a moment and at that time we knew that only because of the Grace that we had been given were we able to give.

We are not church goers, but we are believers. That day showed me the pure Light of God's sweet love. I returned to college, on the last evening of class, with this story in hand. I turned in "my project" and the instructor read it....then she looked up at me and said, "Can I share this?" I slowly nodded as she got the attention of the class. She began to read and that is when I knew that we, as human beings and being part of God. share this need to heal people and be healed.

In my own way I had touched the people at McDonald's, my husband, son, instructor, and every soul that shared the classroom on the last night I spent as a college student. I graduated with one of the biggest lessons I would ever learn....UNCONDITIONAL ACCEPTANCE.

So Much to be Thankful for...
Thanks to Monique Gilbert for forwarding the following.
I am thankful for...
The mess to clean after a party because it means I have been surrounded by friends.
The taxes I pay because it means that I am employed.
The clothes that fit a little too snug because it means I have enough to eat.
All the complaining I hear about government because it means we have freedom of speech.
The lady behind me in church who sings off key because it means that I can hear.
My shadow who watches me work because it means I am out in the sunshine.
The spot I find at the far end of the parking lot because it means I am capable of walking.
The piles of laundry and ironing because it means my loved ones are nearby.
Weariness and aching muscles at the end of the day because it means I have been productive.
A lawn that needs mowing, windows that need cleaning, and gutters that need fixing because it means I have a home.
My huge heating bill because it means I am warm.
The alarm that goes off in the early morning hours because it means that I am alive.

<u>Thanks to Eric Hernandez for forwarding the following.</u>
Thank You God, for Ordinary Days
In the course of our busy days, how often do we focus on the minor annoyances and ignore the blessings that grace our lives?
Thank you, God, for dirty dishes for they mean we are well fed.
Thank you for the mortgage payments and rent notices, for they mean we have a roof over our heads.
Thank you for the seemingly endless pile of laundry, for it means we are clothed and warm.
Thank you, God, for scuff marks and crayon marks and smelly tennis shoes, for they mean our children are healthy and active.
Thank you for loud stereos and busy telephones for they mean our teens are safe at home.
Thank you for the notes from school, for they mean our children have teachers who care.
Thank you, God, for speeding tickets, for they mean our police officers are protecting us.
Thank you for morning traffic jams, for they mean we have jobs to go to.
Thank you for doctor's waiting rooms and deductibles and co-pays, for they mean we have access to health care.
Thank you, God, for his/her snoring, for it means he/she is safe beside me.
Thank you for little disappointments, for they mean you are teaching us patience.
Thank you, God, for ordinary days.

Two artists each painted a picture to illustrate his conception of rest. The first chose for his scene a still, lone lake among the far-off mountains - it was a beautiful and calm scene. The second painted on his canvas a thundering waterfall, with a fragile birch-tree bending

189

over the foam at its base; in the fork of the branch, almost wet with the waterfall's spray, a robin sat on its nest.

The first was only Stagnation; the last was Rest. For in rest there is always two elements - tranquillity and energy; silence and turbulence; creation and destruction; fearless-ness and fearfulness.
- Written by H. Drummond

IT'S NOT EASY:
-to apologize
-to begin over
-to admit error
-to keep trying
-to take advice
-to be unselfish
-to be charitable
-to face a sneer
-to avoid mistakes
-to endure success
-to profit by mistakes
-to keep out of the rut
-to forgive and forget
-to think and then act
-to make the best of little
-to subdue an unruly temper
-to recognize the silver lining
-to shoulder a deserved blame
BUT IT ALWAYS PAYS!!!

From the humor pen of Robert Orben - I hate it when doctors tell you to give up wine, women and song if you don't want to die before your time --particularly when wine, women and song are the reasons why you don't want to die before your time.

<u>On Doing and Being...Anyway</u>
(It is said that Mother Theresa had this on her wall....)
People are often unreasonable, illogical, and self-centered;
Forgive them anyway.
If you are kind, people may accuse you of selfish, ulterior motives;
Be kind anyway.
If you are successful, you will win some false friends and some true enemies;
Succeed anyway.
If you are honest and frank, people may cheat you;
Be honest and frank anyway.
What you spend years building, someone could destroy overnight;
Build anyway.
If you find serenity and happiness, they may be jealous;
Be happy anyway.
The good you do today, people will often forget tomorrow;
Do good anyway.
Give the world the best you have, and it may never be enough;
Give the world the best you've got anyway.
You see, in the final analysis, it is between you and God;
It never was between you and them anyway.

This quote is from the chapter on Lewis and Clark:
"Friendship is different from all other relationships. Unlike an acquaintanceship, it is based on love. Unlike lovers and married couples, it is free of jealousy. Unlike children and parents, it knows neither criticism nor resentment. Friendship has no status in law.

Business partnerships are based on a contract. So is marriage. Parents are bound by the law, as are children. But friendship is freely entered into, freely given, freely exercised.

Friends never cheat each other, or take advantage, or lie. Friends do not spy on one another, yet they have no secrets. Friends glory in each other's successes and are downcast by the failures. Friends minister to each other, nurse each other. Friends give to each other, worry about each other, stand always read to help. Perfect friendship is rarely achieved, but at its height it is an ecstasy."

A Friend --
(A)ccepts you as you are
(B)elieves in "you"
(C)alls you just to say "Hi"
(D)oesn't give up on you
(E)nvisions the whole of you (even the unfinished parts)
(F)orgives your mistakes
(G)ives unconditionally
(H)elps you
(I)nvites you over
(J)ust enjoys being with you
(K)eeps you close at heart
(L)oves you for who you are
(M)akes a difference in your life
(N)ever judges
(O)ffers support
(P)icks you up
(Q)uiets your fears
(R)aises your spirits
(S)ays nice things about you

(T)ells you the truth when you need to hear it
(U)nderstands you
(V)alues you
(W)alks beside you
(X)-plain things you don't understand
(Y)ells when you won't listen, and
(Z)aps you back to reality
Author Unknown

Subject: friends
When you are sad,.............I will dry your tears.
When you are scared,..........I will comfort your fears.
When you are worried,........I will give you hope.
When you are confused,........I will help you cope.
And when you are lost,........And can't see the light.
I shall be your beacon........Shining ever so bright
This is my oath...............I pledge till the end.
Why you may ask?..............Because you're my friend.

Eleanor Roosevelt wrote:
Many people will walk in and out of your life,
But only true friends will leave footprints in your heart.
To handle yourself, use your head; To handle others, use your heart.
Anger is only one letter short of danger.
If someone betrays you once, it is his fault;
If he betrays you twice, it is your fault.
Great minds discuss ideas;
Average minds discuss events;
Small minds discuss people.
He who loses money, loses much;
He who loses a friend, loses much more;
He who loses faith, loses all.

193

Beautiful young people are accidents of nature,
But beautiful old people are works of art.
Learn from the mistakes of others.
You can't live long enough to make them all yourself.
Friends, you and me....
You brought another friend....
And then there were 3....
We started our group....
Our circle of friends....
And like that circle....
There is no beginning or end....

"Information Please"

When I was quite young, my father had one of the first telephones in our neighborhood. I remember well the polished old case fastened to the wall. The shiny receiver hung on the side of the box. I was too little to reach the telephone, but used to listen with fascination when my mother used to talk to it.

Then I discovered that somewhere inside the wonderful device lived an amazing person...her name was Information Please and there was nothing she did not know. Information Please could supply anybody's number and the correct time.

My first personal experience with this genie-in-the bottle came one day while my mother was visiting a neighbor. Amusing myself at the tool bench in the basement, I whacked my finger with a hammer. The pain was terrible, but there didn't seem to be any reason in crying because there was no one home to give sympathy. I walked around the house sucking my throbbing finger, finally arriving at the stairway---the telephone! Quickly I ran for the footstool in the parlor and dragged it to the landing. Climbing up, I unhooked the receiver in the parlor and held it to my ear. "Information please", I said into the mouthpiece just above my head.

A click or two and a small clear voice spoke into my ear. "Information" "I hurt my finger" I wailed into the phone. The tears came readily enough now that I had an audience.

"Isn't your mother home?" came the question.

"Nobody's home but me" I blubbered.

"Are you bleeding?"

"No" I replied, "I hit my finger with the hammer and it hurts"

"Can you open your icebox?" she asked.

I said I could. "Then chip off a little piece of ice and hold it to your finger."

After that I called Information Please for everything. I asked for help with my geography and she told me where Philadelphia was. She helped me with my math, and she told me my pet chipmunk I had caught in the park just the day before would eat fruits and nuts. And there was the time that Petey, our pet canary died. I called Information Please and told her the sad story. She listened, then said the usual things grown-ups say to soothe a child.

"Why is it that birds should sing so beautifully and bring joy to all families only to end up as a heap of feathers up on the bottom of the cage?" She must have sensed my deep concern, for she said quietly, "Paul, always remember that there are other worlds to sing in." Somehow I felt better.

Another day I was on the telephone. "Information Please."

"Information." said the now familiar voice. "How do you spell fix?" I asked.

All of this took place in a small town in the pacific Northwest. Then when I was 9 years old, we moved across the country to Boston. I missed my friend very much. "Information Please" belonged in that old wooden box back home, and I somehow never thought of trying the tall, shiny new phone that sat on the hall table. Yet as I grew into my teens, the memories of those childhood conversations never really left me; often in moments of doubt and perplexity I would recall the serene sense of security I had then. I appreciated now how patient, understanding, and kind she was to have spent her time on a little boy.

A few years later, on my way west to college, my plane put down in Seattle. I had about half an hour or so between planes and I spent 15 minutes or so on the phone with my sister, who lived there now.

Then without thinking what I was doing, I dialed my hometown operator and said, "Information Please."

Miraculously, I heard again the small, clear voice I knew so well, "Information."

I hadn't planned this but I heard myself saying, "Could you tell me please how to spell fix?"

There was a long pause. Then came the soft-spoken answer, "I guess that your finger must have healed by now." I laughed, "So it's really still you," I said. "I wonder if you have any idea how much you meant to me during that time?"

"I wonder, she said, if you know how much your calls meant to me. I never had any children, and I used to look forward to your calls."

I told her how often I had thought of her over the years and I asked if I could call her again when I came back to visit my sister. "Please do, just ask for Sally."

Just three months later I was back in Seattle. A different voice answered "Information" and I asked for Sally. "Are you a friend?"

"Yes, a very old friend."

"Then I'm sorry to have to tell you. Sally has been working part-time the last few years because she was sick. She died five weeks ago." But before I could hang up she said, "Wait a minute. Did you say your name was Paul?"

"Yes."

"Well, Sally left a message for you. She wrote it down. Here it is. I'll read it" "Tell him I still say there are other worlds to sing in. He'll know what I mean"
I thanked her and hung up. I did know what Sally meant.
- Author Unknown

Santa's on his way - maybe? Research has uncovered some shocking facts about Santa Claus and his distribution of presents.
*Excluding non-believers and bad children, Santa must visit over 91.8 million homes within the 31 hours of Christmas Eve darkness afforded by the earth's rotation.
*He must travel at least 72,522,000 miles, not counting ocean crossings.
*Given his 31-hour deadline, he must maintain a speed of 650 miles per second.
*The massive sleigh requires 214,200 reindeer to pull it, increasing the total Santa payload to 353,430 tons.
The 353,430 tons of reindeer and presents traveling at 650 miles per second would create massive heat and air resistance, with the two lead reindeer absorbing 14.3 quintillion joules of energy per second each.

A CHRISTMAS STORY
Paul received a new automobile from his brother as a Christmas present. On Christmas Eve, when Paul came out of his office, a street urchin was walking around the shiny new car, admiring it. "Is this your car, Mister?" he asked.
Paul nodded, "My brother gave it to me for Christmas." The boy was astounded. "You mean your brother gave it to you and it didn't cost you nothing? Boy, I wish..." He hesitated.

And Paul knew what he was going to wish. He was going to wish he had a brother like that. But what the lad said jarred Paul all the way down to his heels.

"I wish," the boy went on, "that I could be a brother like that."

Paul looked at the boy in astonishment, then impulsively he added, "Would you like to ride in my automobile?"

"Oh, yes, I'd love that."

After a short ride, the urchin turned and with his eyes aglow, said, "Mister, would you mind driving in front of my house?"

Paul smiled a little. He thought he knew what the lad wanted. He wanted to show his neighbors that he could ride home in a big automobile. But Paul was wrong again.

"Will you stop where those two steps are?" the boy asked.

He ran up the steps. Then in a little while Paul heard him coming back, but he was not coming fast. He was carrying his little polio-crippled brother. He sat him down on the bottom step, then sort of squeezed up against him and pointed to the car.

"There she is, Buddy, just like I told you upstairs. His brother gave it to him for Christmas and it didn't cost him a cent. And some day I'm gonna give you one just like it...then you can see for yourself all the pretty things in the Christmas windows that I've been trying to tell you about."

Paul got out and lifted the little lad to the front seat of his car. The shining-eyed older brother climbed in beside him and the three of them began a memorable holiday ride.

That Christmas Eve Paul learned what Jesus meant when he said: "It is more blessed to give..."

Attributed to Success Unlimited Magazine

One of the best gifts I ever received was from my daughter, Janna. She gave me a coffee mug with positive sayings wrapped all the way around the cup. Here is what I look at when I use this cup:

"Whatever your mind can conceive and believe, it will achieve. Dream great dreams and make them come true. Do it now. You are unique. In all the history of the world there was never anyone else exactly like you, and in all the infinity to come there will never be another you. Never affirm self-limitations. What you believe yourself to be, you are. To accomplish great things, you must not only act, but also dream; not only plan, but also believe. If you have built castles in the air, your work need not be lost-put foundations under them. Yes you can. Believing is magic. You can always better your best. You don't know what you can do until you try. Nothing will come of nothing. If you don't go out on a limb, you're never going to get the fruit. There is no failure except in no longer trying. Hazy goals produce hazy results. Clearly define your goals. Write them down, make a plan for achieving them, set a deadline, visualize the results and go after them. Just don't look back unless you want to go that way. Defeat may test you, but it need not stop you. If at first you don't succeed, try another way. For every obstacle, there is a solution. Nothing in the world can take the place of persistence. The greatest mistake is giving up. Wishing will not bring success, but planning, persistence and a burning desire will. There is a gold mine within you from which you can extract all the necessary ingredients. Success is an attitude. Get yours right. It is astonishing how short a time it takes for very wonderful things to happen. Now, show us the colors of your rainbow."
Success/Barbara Smallwood and Steve Kilborn

The cup is truly an inspiration and a great way to start the day!!!

Only those who will risk going too far can possibly find out how far one can go. - T. S. Eliot

May you always find new roads to travel; new horizons to explore; and new dreams to call your own. - Hal Roach

Great Gulps
Of
Gusto

**"A hero is an ordinary individual
who finds the strength
to persevere and endure
in spite of
overwhelming obstacles."
- Christopher Reeve**

How do you read the following: OPPORTUNITYISNOWHERE - see below for the two ways to interpret this.

As we approach a new day, month or year, look upon it with positive eyes, positive attitude and a positive belief that this will be the best yet for yourself and those you love. Here's an affirmative statement to read to yourself each day.

I stand at the gate of the year, gratefully looking back upon the old, eager to move forward into the new.
I joyously look forward to this year.
Each day promises new happiness.
My eyes are opened to possibilities that former fears and doubts prevented me from seeing.
My life is transformed by the renewing of my mind.
Behold my thinking makes all things new!
I stand strong in the face of adverse circumstances, feeling the presence of a miracle-working power.
My life is an exciting adventure filled with opportunities and rewards.
I am relaxed and at ease, a pleasure to be around, never fussy or fretful about little things.
I forgive myself for all past mistakes.
Today I will practice loving myself and releasing any feelings of guilt.
Whatever fears I may have had are gone.
If God is with me, of whom or what could I be afraid?
My life has infinite possibilities.
Today I share my strength with those who are fearful and confused, they will know they have my complete support.

I stand in awe of the changes that are taking place.
I accept the truth that nothing can limit me in any way.
Today everything is made new because I break out of my shell of self-limitation!
I give thanks for the loving care and protection that is with me every moment.

Which do you see? (1) OPPORTUNITY IS NOW HERE or
(2) OPPORTUNITY IS NOWHERE. Let's hope it is number one.

ON TIME FLIES
The transitory mayfly
Is anxious to spawn,
For it knows in two hours
It's gonna pass on.
If you knew your life span
Were equally meager,
I imagine you, too,
Would tend to be eager.
-Paul Richards

EVERYDAY SURVIVAL KIT
Toothpick
Rubber Band
Band Aid
Pencil
Eraser
Chewing Gum
Mint
Candy Kiss
Tea Bag

HERE'S WHY:

Toothpick -- to remind you to pick out the good qualities in others

Rubber Band -- to remind you to be flexible, things might not always go the way you want, but it will work out

Band Aid -- To remind you to heal hurt feelings, yours or someone else's

Pencil -- To remind you to list your blessings everyday

Eraser -- To remind you that everyone makes mistakes, and it's OK

Chewing Gum -- To remind you to stick with it, you can accomplish anything

Mint -- To remind you that you are worth a mint to your family and friends

Candy Kiss -- To remind you that everyone needs a kiss & a hug everyday including you

Tea Bag -- To remind you to relax daily and go over that list of your blessings

To the world, you may just be somebody....but to somebody you may be the world.

GOALS

1. What are the 5 things you value most in life?
2. In 30 seconds, write down the 3 most important goals in your life right now.
3. What would you do if you won a million dollars in the lottery tomorrow? How would you spend it?
4. What would you do and how would you spend your time if you learned today that you have only 6 months to live?
5. What have you always wanted to do but have been afraid to attempt?
6. In looking back over all the things you've done in your life - what type of activities, doing what sort of things, in what sort of

circumstances, gives you your greatest feeling of importance, mental well-being, high self-esteem and high self-worth?

7. You have one wish or a magic pill - what one great thing would you dare to dream if you knew you could not fail?

Ask questions:
Where will this road lead?
What if this becomes a habit?
What if others imitate me?
What if my children follow in my footsteps?
What if the whole world lived this way?
What if everyone were just like me?
If you keep following the path you're on, where will you end up?

Health Plan for 21st century - The best way to stay healthy is to eat what you don't want, drink what you don't like and do what you'd rather not.

Often people attempt to live their lives backwards: they try to have more things, or more money, in order to do more of what they want so they will be happier. The way it actually works is the reverse. You must first be who you really are, then, do what you need to do, in order to have what you want. - Margaret Young

HOW TO BECOME THE PERSON YOU WANT TO BE
- Henry J. Kaiser

1. Know yourself and decide what you want most of all to make out of your life. Then write down your goals and a plan to reach them.
2. Use the great powers you can tap through faith in God and the hidden energies of your soul and subconscious mind.
3. Love people and serve them.

4. Develop your positive traits of character and personality.
5. Work! Put your life's plan into determined action and go after what you want with all that's in you.

In today's economy there are no experts, no 'best and brightest' with all the answers. It's up to each one of us. The only way to screw up is to not try anything. - Thomas J. Peters

HOW TO PROFIT FROM YOUR MISTAKES - Douglas Lurton
1. You profit by facing mistakes squarely. Don't alibi.
2. You profit if you don't let mistakes get you down.
3. You profit if you learn how to take criticism.
4. You profit most by learning from your own mistakes and those of others.
5. You learn by taking courage from the fact that others, even the famous, make mistakes also.

You don't always get what you ask for, but you never get what you don't ask for... unless it's contagious! - Franklyn Broude

The American Medical Association tells us that we must learn to control our thoughts and then think right. It lists eight excellent rules for us to follow:
1. Quit looking for a knock in your motor.
2. Learn to like your work.
3. Have at least one hobby.
4. Learn to like people.
5. Learn to be satisfied when you can't easily change your situation.
6. Learn to accept adversity.
7. School yourself to learn to say the cheerful, helpful and humorous thing.

8. Learn to face your challenges and your problems with confidence and decision.

It is health that is real wealth and not pieces of gold and silver.
- Mahatma Gandhi

HOW TO REBUILD YOUR BODY - Ed Sainsbury
1. Walk two miles a day.
2. Perform your own calisthenics before breakfast and before bedtime.
3. Take a cool bath six days a week, a short hot bath on the seventh day, with a brisk rub after each.
4. Play golf or take a long hike, once a week.
5. Eat fewer fried and starchy food; eat more fruit, vegetables and proteins.

The sun is always shining. Even though clouds may come along and obscure the sun for a while, the sun is always shining. The sun never stops shining. And even though the earth turns, and the sun appears to go down, it really never stops shining. - Louise L. Hay

The yard sale I had this last weekend went much better than I expected.
I made a fortune! And not once did any of my family members throw themselves on an item screaming, "No! Don't buy that! I need it!" Mostly they just stood around, sighed a lot and looked very pained.
It turns out it was me that had a problem selling some of the items. But it wasn't until a woman offered me a nickel for one of the children's book that I lost it. This wasn't just any old book you see. This was "Green Eggs and Ham"! I must have read that book a

thousand times to each of my children over the years. Sometimes I would even fix them that very thing for dinner (with the help of a little green food coloring. My cooking is not that bad!

This book was priceless! Without even realizing I was going to do it I heard myself say, "I'm sorry, I have decided not to sell this one."

"I'll give you ten cents for it and not a cent more!

It's only a kids' book," she told me curtly.

Looking into her scowling face I could not resist asking,

"Have you ever eaten green eggs and ham?" "Of course not!" she sputtered. "What a stupid question!" And with that said she made a final, less than kind comment and stormed out of the garage.

As I sat there feeling a bit silly about the whole thing I heard a small voice next to me say, "I have never eaten green eggs and ham, but I would!" Turning I looked into the smiling face of a little girl of about four.

"Would you eat them in a box?" I asked her. She grinned,

"I would eat them in a box and with a fox!" Then her little hand opened to reveal one shiny penny. "Is this enough for the book?"

"Well, there is a small problem," I told her. "If I sell you Sam-I-Am, then Horton and the Cat in the Hat and all the others would be so lonely and sad. Do you think you could take them too?"

"Oh, I could take them all! I really could!"

Her mother thanked me profusely as she helped her daughter gather up the books. Asking her to hold on a minute, I dashed into the house and returned and handed the mother a small bottle. Laughing as she gazed at the small green bottle, she told me, "Looks like I will have to stop at the store and get some ham and eggs."

The penny now sits in my memory box, forever a reminder of the true cost of something priceless.

See, I told you I made a fortune! - Author Unknown

<u>From the pen of Tom Haggai -</u>

If you ever feel you have too much to accomplish each day; if you ever feel swamped and unable to keep ahead of your workload; if you sleep soundly but wake up more fatigued because of these pressures, the solution could be improved time management. The following ideas may help you better plan and organize your time:

1. <u>Identify your goals</u> - Just knowing what needs to be done is not enough - you must arrange priorities. You need to differentiate tasks that <u>must</u> be done from those that <u>should</u> be done if possible. If you are an employer, for instance, your primary obligation is to your employees. Yet you also have time commitments as a member of various civic, charitable and social organizations. You must guard against being over-involved in worthwhile activities that impair your leadership responsibility to your company and its employees.

2. <u>Write down your goals</u> - Jot down major goals for your job, such as sales targets, as well as the little things you do before and after work. Depending on your personal choice, you might want to make your list each night before retiring or each morning upon arising. Then, as you complete each task, check it off and feel the sense of accomplishment.

3. <u>Accept the unexpected</u> - Any goal is subject to the unexpected. Don't be discouraged by occasional detours or changes. Accept the unexpected as a matter of life, or even the spice of life that adds excitement to our existence. If you miss a goal, write yourself a note explaining why, and go right ahead from there.

4. <u>Don't look behind you</u> - If you are having a good day, don't fret about the bad day you had yesterday. If a task blew up in your face yesterday, don't let it haunt you today.

5. <u>Be honest with yourself</u> - Learn the difference between deliberation and procrastination. There are times when haste can make waste, but there are also times when delay can turn a small, insignificant task into one of gigantic proportions.

Learning to manage time effectively is the first step in eliminating that "the faster I go, the behinder I get" feeling. But you still may need to lighten your load. Don't allow pride and ego to keep you from admitting that you have more work than you can handle effectively.

Thanks to Tim Buckley

I was reading an article in the September issue of *Reader's Digest* entitled "A Question of Trust" by Sherry Hemman Hogan and came across a couple of sentences which grabbed me. One is credited to Emerson, "All I have seen teaches me to trust the Creator for all I have not seen." The other is the author's, "Leaps of faith can be very good exercise for the healing heart."

Although I wish I had thought to say those things, I didn't. But I can pass them on, because I think they are worth sharing.

Thanks to Susan Arnold...

BEAUTY TIPS FOR THE "INNER YOU"

For attractive lips, speak words of kindness.

For beautiful eyes, seek out the good in other people.

To lose weight, let go of stress and the need to control others.

To improve your ears, listen to the word of God.

For poise, walk with knowledge and self-esteem.

To strengthen your arms, hug at least three people a day.

To strengthen your heart, forgive yourself and others.

Touch someone with your love.

Rather than focus upon the thorns of life, smell the roses and count your blessings.

Don't worry and hurry so much ...

Rather walk this earth lightly and yet leave your mark!

<u>Thanks to my daughter for a similar comment:</u>
The following was written by Audrey Hepburn regarding "Beauty Tips".
For attractive lips, speak words of kindness.
For lovely eyes, seek out the good in people.
For a slim figure, share your food with the hungry.
For beautiful hair, let a child run his or her fingers through it once a day.
For poise, walk with the knowledge that you'll never walk alone.

and.....
People, even more than things, have to be restored, renewed, revived, reclaimed, and redeemed; never throw out anybody.
Remember, if you ever need a helping hand, you'll find one at the end of your arm. As you grow older, you will discover that you have two hands, one for helping yourself and one for helping others.
(Author unknown)

<u>Thanks to: Livingstone Kumassah for "Words To Live By"</u>
1. Anger is a condition in which the tongue works faster than the mind.
2. You can't change the past, but you can ruin the present by worrying over the future.
3. Love ......and you shall be loved.
4. God always gives His best to those who leave the choice with Him.
5. All people smile in the same language.
6. A hug is a great gift--one size fits all. It can be given for any occasion...and it's easy to exchange.
7. Everyone needs to be loved...especially when they do not deserve it.

211

8. The real measure of a man's wealth is what he has invested in eternity.
9. Laughter is God's sunshine.
10. Everything has beauty but not everyone sees it.
11. It's important for parents to live the same things they teach.
12. Thank God for what you have, TRUST GOD for what you need.
13. If you fill your heart with regrets of yesterday and the worries of tomorrow, you have no today to be thankful for.
14. Happy memories never wear out--relive them as often as you want.
15. Home is the place where we grumble the most, but are often treated the best.
16. Man looks at outward appearance but the Lord looks within.
17. The choice you make today will usually affect tomorrow.
18. Take time to laugh for it is the music of the soul.
19. If anyone speaks badly of you, live so none will believe it.
20. Patience is the ability to idle your motor when you feel like stripping your gears.
21. Love is strengthened by working through conflicts together.
22. The best thing parents can do for their children is to love each other.
23. Harsh words break no bones but they do break hearts.
24. To get out of a difficulty, one usually must go through it.
25. We take for granted the things that we should be giving thanks for.
26. Love is the only thing that can be divided without being diminished.
27. Happiness is enhanced by others but does not depend upon others.
28. You are richer today if you have laughed, given or forgiven.
29. For every minute you are angry with someone, you lose 60 seconds of happiness that you can never get back.

30. Do what you can, for who you can, with what you have, and where you are.

31. The best gifts to give:

To Your friend -- loyalty;

To your enemy -- forgiveness;

To your boss -- service;

To a child -- a good example;

To your parents -- gratitude and devotion;

To your mate - love and faithfulness;

To all men and women - charity; and

To God - your life

The difference between ordinary and extraordinary is the <u>extra</u>.

That certain something that makes us great, that pulls us out of the mediocre and commonplace, that builds into us power. It glows and shines, it lights up our faces. Its that something extra called - ENTHUSIASM.

Enthusiasm - the keynote that makes us sing and makes others sing with us.

Enthusiasm - the maker of friends, the maker of smiles, the producer of confidence. It cries to the world, "I've got what it takes." It tells everyone that our job is a good job, that our work suits us fine, that I'm glad I have a job and the talents I have are the best.

Enthusiasm - the inspiration that makes us "Wake Up and Live." It puts spring in our step, spring in our hearts, a twinkle in our eyes and gives us confidence in ourselves and our fellow man.

Enthusiasm - changes an uninspired worker into a producer, a pessimist into an optimist, a loafer into a go-getter.

Enthusiasm - is the vibrant thrill in your voice that sways the will of others into harmony with your own.

Enthusiasm - if you have it, you should thank God for it. If you don't have it, you should get down on your knees and pray for it.
-Author Unknown

Don't complain about what you don't have. Use what you've got. To do less than your best is a sin. Every single one of us has the power for greatness, because greatness is determined by service -- to yourself and to others. - Oprah Winfrey

Although business oriented, the following can apply to the business of life in first seeking to understand others and what people really want in life!
What people really want in an age when…
-business
-profits
-performance
-productivity
-busyness
-sales
-satisfied customers
-competition
-share holder value
-low sales costs
-low margins…
…seem to be driving organizations to all time high - stress levels, employee burn-out, a lack of employee loyalty and their having less overall concern for the health and well- being of the organization as a whole, it would seem that someone out there in management-land would finally get the idea that all of these, are the results of employees who feel either the positive or negative side of feeling: valuable, worthwhile, appreciated and important.

We are in a economic period where employees (people) are saying no - to previous management styles, philosophies and cultures that steal their sense of worth, identity and freedom and yes to, independence, the need for an empowered culture, and involvement to get the job done the way it makes the most sense to them. There are a number of things that employees want. The list is endless. Most managers place money and benefits at the top of the list of employee wants and or concerns. Most employees put; appreciation, recognition, involvement in decisions that directly impact them and a general feeling of 'being in on things.'

We could sum up all of the people wants into just one: Today - People want to feel a sense of belonging. They ask themselves, how do I fit in here? Do I want to fit in here? What will it take to fit in here? How much of myself will I have to give up to fit in here?

Ask yourself, as a manager, the same question and recognize that each of your employees are asking the same questions everyday. As a manager, how are you contributing to their answers?

Management quote for the week: Seek first to understand, then be understood. - S. Covey

We all walk in the dark and each of us must learn to turn on his or her own light. - Earl Nightingale

But perhaps we can turn on the light for others with love, caring and compassion. For those of you that have experienced a death in the family, the following story should bring a feeling of warmth and possibly help with the closure.

ROSES

Red roses were her favorites, her name was also Rose. And every year her husband sent them, tied with pretty bows.

The year he died, the roses were delivered to her door. The card said, "Be my Valentine," like all the years before. Each year he sent her roses, and the note would always say, "I love you even more this year, than last year on this day. My love for you will always grow, with every passing year."

She knew this was the last time that the roses would appear. She thought, he ordered roses in advance before this day. Her loving husband did not know, that he would pass away. He always liked to do things early, way before the time. Then, if he got too busy, everything would work out fine. She trimmed the stems, and placed them in a very special vase. Then, sat the vase beside the portrait of his smiling face. She would sit for hours, in her husband's favorite chair. While staring at his picture, and the roses sitting there. A year went by, and it was hard to live without her mate. With loneliness and solitude, that had become her fate. Then, the very hour, as on Valentines before, the doorbell rang, and there were roses, sitting by her door. She brought the roses in, and then just looked at them in shock. Then, went to get the telephone, to call the florist shop. The owner answered, and she asked him, if he would explain, why would someone do this to her, causing her such pain? "I know your husband passed away, more than a year ago,"

The owner said, "I knew you'd call, and you would want to know. The flowers you received today, were paid for in advance. Your husband always planned ahead, he left nothing to chance. There is a standing order, that I have on file down here, and he has paid, well in advance, you'll get them every year. There also is another thing, that I think you should know, he wrote a special little card...he did this years ago. Then, should it ever happen that he's no longer here, that's the card...that should be sent, to you the following year."

216

She thanked him and hung the phone, her tears now flowing hard. Her fingers shaking, as she slowly reached to get the card. Inside the card, she saw that he had written her a note. Then, as she stared in total silence, this is what he wrote..."Hello my love, I know it's been a year since I've been gone, I hope it hasn't been too hard for you to overcome. I know it must be lonely, and the pain is very real. Or if it was the other way, I know how I would feel. The love we shared made everything so beautiful in life. I loved you more than words can say, you were the perfect wife. You were my friend and lover, you fulfilled my every need. I know it's only been a year, but please try not to grieve. I want you to be happy, even when you shed your tears. That is why the roses will be sent to you for years. When you get these roses, think of all the happiness, that we had together, and how both of us were blessed. I have always loved you and I know I always will. But, my love, you must go on, you have some living still. Please...try to find happiness, while living out your days. I know it is not easy, but I hope you find some ways. The roses will come every year, and they will only stop, when your door's not answered, when the florist stops to knock. He will come five times that day, in case you have gone out. But after his last visit, he will know without a doubt, to take the roses to the place, where I've instructed him. And place the roses where we are, together once again.

Sometimes in life, you find a special friend; someone who changes your life just by being part of it. Someone who makes you laugh until you can't stop; someone who makes you believe that there really is good in the world. Someone who convinces you that there really is an unlocked door just waiting for you to open it.

Is there someone you need to send roses to today?

Don't wait until it's too late. Give them the roses while they still have the chance to appreciate them.

Love does not consist in gazing at each other, but in looking together in the same direction. - Antoine De Saint-Exupery

Learning is finding out what you already know. Doing is demonstrating that you know it. Teaching is reminding others that they know it just as well as you. You are all learners, doers, teachers. - Richard Bach

A SHORT COURSE IN WORK RELATIONS
The six most important words:
I admit I made a mistake.
The five most important words:
You did a great job.
The four most important words:
What do you think?
The three most important words:
Could you please...
The two most important words:
Thank you.
The one most important word:
We

There is no such thing as can't, only won't. If you're qualified, all it takes is a burning desire to accomplish, to make a change. Go forward, go backward. Whatever it takes! But you can't blame other people or society in general. It all comes from your mind. When we do the impossible we realize we are special people.- Jan Ashford

MAKE A PEARL
Most of us can afford to take a lesson from the oyster. The most extraordinary thing about the oyster is this: Irritants get into his shell. He does not like them; he tries to get rid of them. But when he

cannot get rid of them, he settles down to make one of the most beautiful things in the world. He uses the irritation to do the loveliest thing that an oyster ever has a chance to do. If there are irritations in our lives today, there is only one prescription...make a pearl! It may have to be a pearl of patience, but, anyhow, make a pearl. And it takes faith and love to do it. - Harry E. Fosdick

So much of what we intend to do is going to be done tomorrow. In a sense it can be said that tomorrow will be the most wonderful day in history, for that is the day when most of us are going to begin to do better. But today is the "tomorrow" that you looked at yesterday. You could begin today to do better and be better...why put it off? You'll never find a better day than today to begin to be what you've always wanted to be, to begin to live your dream instead of just dreaming it. Don't allow your desires to become museum pieces!

A tree is known by its fruit; a man by his deeds. A good deed is never lost; he who sows courtesy reaps friendship, and he who plants kindness gathers love. - St. Basil

Seven Virtues We Could All Use To Improve Our Lives -
1. Prudence - the ability to regulate and discipline one's self through the exercise of reason.
2. Fortitude - the endurance of physical or mental hardships of suffering without giving way under strain. It is firmness of mind in meeting adversity, resolute endurance, courage and staying power. It is the possession of the stamina essential to face that which repels or frightens us, or to put up with the hardships of a job. It implies triumph. Synonyms are grit, backbone, pluck and guts.
3. Temperance - habitual moderation in the indulgence of our appetites and passions.
4. Justice - the principle of dealing fairly with each other - integrity.

5. Faith - Trust in your maker.
6. Hope - the desire with the expectation of obtaining what is desired or the belief that it is obtainable.
7. Charity - the act of loving each other as brothers and sisters, because we are all children of God. It stresses benevolence and goodwill in giving and in the broad understanding of others with kindly tolerance.
These virtues are all taught in *the Bible, the Talmud, the Book of Mormons, Science and Health with Key to the Scriptures* and almost all inspirational literature - So there must be something to applying them in your life.

It is not what we read, but what we remember that makes us learned. It is not what we intend but what we do that makes us useful. And, it is not a few faint wishes, but a lifelong struggle that makes us valiant.
- Henry Ward Beecher

We celebrate our 100th issue with this story about the joy and love of life and how we need to cherish our time here on earth.

A Sandpiper To Bring You Joy
She was six years old when I first met her on the beach near where I live. I drive to this beach, a distance of three or four miles, whenever the world begins to close in on me. She was building a sandcastle or something and looked up, her eyes as blue as the sea.
"Hello," she said.
I answered with a nod, not really in the mood to bother with a small child.
"I'm building," she said.
"I see that. What is it?" I asked, not caring.
"Oh, I don't know, I just like the feel of sand."

"That sounds good", I thought, and slipped off my shoes. A sandpiper glided by.

"That's a joy," the child said.

"It's a what?"

"It's a joy. My mama says sandpipers come to bring us joy."

The bird went gliding down the beach. "Good-bye joy," I muttered to myself, "hello pain," and turned to walk on. I was depressed; my life seemed completely out of balance.

"What's your name?" She wouldn't give up.

"Robert," I answered. "I'm Robert Peterson."

"Mine's Wendy... I'm six."

"Hi, Wendy."

She giggled. "You're funny," she said.

In spite of my gloom I laughed too and walked on. Her musical giggle followed me.

"Come again, Mr. P," she called. "We'll have another happy day."

The days and weeks that followed belong to others: A group of unruly Boy Scouts, PTA meetings, an ailing mother. The sun was shining one morning as I took my hands out of the dishwater. "I need a sandpiper," I said to myself, gathering up my coat. The ever-changing balm of the seashore awaited me.

The breeze was chilly, but I strode along, trying to recapture the serenity I needed. I had forgotten the child and was startled when she appeared.

"Hello, Mr. P," she said. "Do you want to play?"

"What did you have in mind?" I asked, with a twinge of annoyance.

"I don't know, you say."

"How about charades?" I asked sarcastically.

The tinkling laughter burst forth again. "I don't know what that is."

"Then let's just walk." Looking at her, I noticed the delicate fairness of her face. "Where do you live?" I asked.

221

"Over there." She pointed toward a row of summer cottages. Strange, I thought, in winter. "Where do you go to school?"

"I don't go to school. Mommy says we're on vacation."

She chattered little girl talk as we strolled up the beach, but my mind was on other things. When I left for home, Wendy said it had been a happy day. Feeling surprisingly better, I smiled at her and agreed.

Three weeks later, I rushed to my beach in a state of near panic. I was in no mood to even greet Wendy. I thought I saw her mother on the porch and felt like demanding she keep her child at home.

"Look, if you don't mind," I said crossly when Wendy caught up with me, "I'd rather be alone today."

She seems unusually pale and out of breath.

"Why?" she asked.

I turned to her and shouted, "Because my mother died!" and thought, "My God, why was I saying this to a little child?"

"Oh," she said quietly, "then this is a bad day."

"Yes," I said, "and yesterday and the day before and-oh, go away!"

"Did it hurt?" she inquired.

"Did what hurt?" I was exasperated with her, with myself.

"When she died?"

"Of course it hurt!!!!" I snapped, misunderstanding, wrapped up in myself. I strode off.

A month or so after that, when I next went to the beach, she wasn't there. Feeling guilty, ashamed and admitting to myself I missed her, I went up to the cottage after my walk and knocked at the door. A drawn looking young woman with honey-colored hair opened the door.

"Hello," I said. "I'm Robert Peterson. I missed your little girl today and wondered where she was."

"Oh yes, Mr. Peterson, please come in. Wendy spoke of you so much. I'm afraid I allowed her to bother you. If she was a nuisance, please, accept my apologies."

"Not at all-she's a delightful child," I said, suddenly realizing that I meant it.

"Where is she?"

"Wendy died last week, Mr. Peterson. She had leukemia. Maybe she didn't tell you."

Struck dumb, I groped for a chair. My breath caught.

"She loved this beach; so when she asked to come, we couldn't say no.

She seemed so much better here and had a lot of what she called "happy days."

But the last few weeks, she declined rapidly..." her voice faltered.

"She left something for you... if only I can find it. Could you wait a moment while I look?"

I nodded stupidly, my mind racing for something, anything, to say to this lovely young woman. She handed me a smeared envelope, with MR. P printed in bold, childish letters. Inside was a drawing in bright crayon hues - a yellow beach, a blue sea, and a brown bird. Underneath was carefully printed: A SANDPIPER TO BRING YOU JOY. Tears welled up in my eyes, and a heart that had almost forgotten to love opened wide. I took Wendy's mother in my arms.

"I'm so sorry, I'm sorry, I'm so sorry," I muttered over and over, and we wept together.

The precious little picture is framed now and hangs in my study. Six words - one for each year of her life - that speak to me of harmony, courage, undemanding love. A gift from a child with sea-blue eyes and hair the color of sand-who taught me the gift of love.

NOTE:

The above is a true story sent out by Robert Peterson. It serves as a reminder to all of us that we need to take time to enjoy living and life and each other. "The price of hating other human beings is loving oneself less. Life is so complicated, the hustle and bustle of everyday traumas, can make us lose focus about what is truly important or what

223

is only a momentary setback or crisis. This week, be sure to give your loved ones an extra hug, and by all means, take a moment... even if it is only ten seconds, to stop and smell the roses.

Secrets
of the
Richest
People

**"The more you do,
the more you are."
- Angie Papadakis**

EXTRA ADDED KNOWLEDGE -LAGNIAPPE

Secrets Of The Richest People

Would you like to realize your goals? Maybe you'd like to run your own business, expand your material possessions or succeed in the arts. There is no one path to the pot of gold but many people of all backgrounds have successfully found it.

Whether you want to follow the ways of the great financiers, the famous politicians or the dynamic movie stars, there are some common modes of behavior each of them followed. And in many cases, they have shared their secrets so YOU CAN FOLLOW THEIR FOOTSTEPS.

"If you wish to know the road up the mountain, as the person who goes back and forth on it," said the ancient sage, Zenrin. What better way is there to know the secrets than to ask those who made it?

What goals do you want to achieve? And what amount of effort can you commit? You may want money for the extra things in life, money to build a corporate empire or money to support yourself while you pursue the fine arts.

Perhaps you'd like to take the risk to start something new in your life. You may want to open your own business, devote your energies to an artistic career such as acting, or reap the benefits of your yearly endeavors with fabulous vacations several times a year.

What will bring you happiness? The satisfaction of success takes many forms. Not only are people seeking financial fortunes, but also the ancient goal of peace of mind.

226

Do you worry? You might be concerned about your health or your family's well-being. You may be anxious about the added expenses of education, medical bills or the steady increase of the cost of living.

There are ways out of the endless cycles of worry, stress and anxiety. Right now, you can rise above the whirl of survival to achieve the accomplishments you dream of. When you're ready to put your whole effort into realizing your goals - YOU WILL SUCCEED!!!

What Are Riches?

"Had I but plenty of money, money enough to spare," wrote Robert Browning. And money is the greatest attribute of riches. A universal desire, money is the materialization of riches, the stuff that makes the rest possible.

Are you looking for financial security? For retirement, for education or leisure? Riches are the overflowing abundance of material possessions -- houses, cars, boats, furnishings -- everything you have ever wanted.

Centuries ago, Horace wrote, "By right means, if you can, but by any means, make money." For many people it is a path towards happiness, a cure-all for worry and peace of mind.

For others, riches come in the form of satisfaction and personal independence. Satisfaction comes from accomplishment in employment or attaining goals. It is that feeling of contentment and confidence from a good task well done.

Riches are closely linked with success. And with that comes fame and acknowledgment of position. Success might be the feeling of well-being from the rewards of good effort. Or the enthusiasm and vitality triggered by recognition.

"Success is how well I enjoy the minutes," said producer Norman Lear.

Throughout history, the people who lived with riches often achieved them by hard work, diligence and a belief in themselves. For some people, it took courage, genius and stamina.

But for many others, it took nothing special but the desire to turn dreams into reality. Whether you want millions of dollars, recognition as an artist or personal freedom, you have the ability to make your life as rich as you want.

Think about what you desire most. It may not be hard cash, but what the hard cash can buy. Or it may be those feelings of inner satisfaction, from creating something beautiful or strong.

You may want personal independence from the work week or freedom to live anywhere you want. You may be looking for something meaningful and significant in life -- something other than things money can buy.

Whatever your goals and however difficult they seem to be to accomplish, you have the ability to become who you want. Take a look -- can you see yourself surrounded by riches.

Picture the world open and in front of you, ready to become the form of your dreams, ready to stage your desires. "Why then, the world's mine oyster, " wrote William Shakespeare, "which I, with sword, will open."

Who Is Successful?

Many people who achieve fortune in the world are not born rich. But they accomplish their desires through hard work and a plan of action.

Every type of person on earth can become successful. There are saints and scoundrels; philanthropists and thieves; poets and politicians; young and old. There are no limitations or physical boundaries for success.

Success comes to those who think about success and strive for it. Although many rich financiers at the turn of the century had no formal education, they overcame that and went on to great fame.

Some people strive towards a single goal from early in life and often attain that goal while still young. Others are willing to risk new adventures later and still attain success.

"It's never too late to learn," wrote Malcolm Forbes, the money magnate. "I learned to ride a motorcycle at age 50 and fly hot-air balloons at age 52."

Whatever your task, whatever your obstacles, you can be as successful as anyone else. Study the people who accomplished recognition in the areas of your pursuit. How did they achieve their goals?

And don't be afraid that you don't have what it takes. As Daniel Webster wrote, "There is always room at the top."

Forming Convictions

The single attribute that every successful person has is the one-pointed devotion to attain a goal. "There in the sunshine are my highest aspirations," wrote Louisa May Alcott, "I can look up and see their beauty, believe in them and try to follow where they lead."

What are your desires? How can you form them into definite goals that you can attain? Lawrence Peter wrote, "If you don't know where you're going, you'll probably end up somewhere else."

Maybe you're studying a craft or skill. Perhaps you're caught in a rung of the corporate ladder. Or you might feel constricted by your family and the environment around you.

Which star are you reaching for? "Ours is a world where people don't know what they want and are willing to go through anything to get it," wrote Don Marquis.

Take the time to think about your own aspirations. Look inside to find what feels right. Almost everyone entertains the notions of fame and fortune but you need to put on the costume that fits you.

Conviction requires certain qualities of action. You must be sincere and be willing to assume responsibility. And you need the self-discipline necessary to work towards your goals.

Are you prepared to achieve your dreams? Can you form their reality in your mind? Will you devote your entire being to attaining what you want?

On Your Own

Most millionaires are non-conformists. So are the most famous actors and actresses and the most prominent artists. Writers are known for their individual traits and eccentricities.

Your convictions and goals are your own business, even when you find help along the path. Mentors often take people under their wings to nourish and teach. Or spiritual guides will show you the path to attainment. But you're on your own to achieve.

Cultivate a sense of justice and an ability to make decisions. Cooperate with everybody and develop your own self-respect. And follow good criticism and advice after you've judged carefully. J.Paul Getty said, "I advise young millionaires to be skeptical of advice. They should advise themselves, they should form their own opinions."

Lord Byron wrote, "There is rapture on the lonely shore.' And if you attain your goals with poise and sincerity, you'll find warmth and love at the top - not the cold loneliness pictured by the jealous.

Put on blinders to negative comments and criticism meant to hurt you. About the people who criticize, Voltaire wrote, "Never having been able to succeed in the world, they took revenge by speaking ill of it."

Carpae Diem - Seize The Day

People are judged by what they think and what they say. But the true measure of their character is what they do. Anyone who has achieved success and fortune in the world has done it by action.

William Jennings Bryan wrote, "Destiny is not a matter of chance, it is a matter of choices; it is not a thing to be waited for, it is a thing to be achieved."

The choice of the path you follow is often put before you as opportunity. "Few people recognize opportunity," said Cary Grant, "because it comes disguised as hard work."

Don't let opportunities slip past while you're still considering them and create new ones as you see them. "Wise people make more opportunities than they find."

What opportunities can you act upon? Woolworth saw a need for small inexpensive items and opened the chain of stores that grossed billions. Wrigley started giving gum away as a bonus from a supplies wagon he sold from and saw the opportunity to make money from the gum that became in high demand.

All successful people the world over have found the opportunities for their own special talents and acted upon those ways to achieve. Why wait for the time to pass? There's never a better time than now.

"Sometimes," wrote Lewis Carroll, "I've believed as many as six impossible things before breakfast." Take your own impossible dreams and make them become reality.

How They Think

Thousands of potential millionaires are born every year. And making a million dollars is coming closer to everyone's pocket. What advice did the money-makers follow?

Aristotle Onassis worked 18 hours a day to maintain his fortune. He started as a welder and aimed for the top. "You have to think money day and night," he said, "you should even dream about it in your sleep."

John D. Rockefeller, Jr., said, "I believe in the dignity of labor, whether with head or hand; that the world owes every person an opportunity to make a living." He didn't say that the world owed everybody a living - only an opportunity.

And J.Paul Getty acknowledged his hard work: "I have no complex about wealth. I have worked hard for my money, producing things people need."

Even Proverbs advises: "In all labor there is profit."

Richard Bach, the author of the best selling "Jonathan Livingston Seagull" wrote, "You are never given a wish without also being given the power to make it true. You may have to work for it, however."

The Empress of the British Empire, Queen Victoria, admonished, "We are not interested in the possibilities of defeat."

Do You Have What It Takes?

There are qualities of endeavor and achievement that are common to many people who make it to the top. The following questions are a guideline to self-enterprise and attaining your goals:
1. Do you prefer to work for yourself than for others?
2. Are you well-informed on current business & political affairs?
3. Are you a leader?
4. Do you take advantage of opportunities?
5. Do you pay attention to what other people say?
6. Can you finish a job even when it is difficult or unpleasant?
7. Are you challenged by problems?
8. Do you have a goal you want to achieve?
9. Do you consider other people?

10. Do you strive to attain?
11. Can you obey commands?
12. Can you bounce back after defeats?
13. Do you believe in yourself?
14. Can you stand by your actions in spite of criticism?
15. Can you follow instructions?
16. Can you respond to the needs of others?
17. Will you give credit to others?
18. Can you make your own decisions?
19. Are you determined?
20. Are you ready for success?

Establish A Goal

What do you want? Are you looking for financial security, professional acknowledgment, spiritual attainment? Do you want to fit better socially or become more expressive creatively? Establish a goal that's right for you.

The Beginning

Take a look at yourself -- inside and out. Where do you live, what job do you have, how do you relate to your friends and family? What interests do you pursue, what adventures do you have?

What do you truly want from life? Do you want wealth and success, happiness and peace of mind? Do you want a family, nice home, possibly a yacht or a sports car? Where are you going? Do you have a particular goal or are you just wandering through life?

You can accomplish anything you want in life -- that's true. Once you have a particular goal, you can fulfill that desire by straightforward commitment and total conviction.

But what if you don't know what you want? Maybe your goals are small ones -- like loosing some weight, or buying a new car. Maybe getting a promotion or finding a mate.

Whether you want a bigger apartment or want to be a corporation president, any avenue of prosperity and achievement is open to you if it is truly what you want.

No goal is too small; no dream is too big. And even if you aren't clear on your desires, you can tap into your subconscious mind to get the answers and to find the paths to success.

Can you change your life -- do you want to? Can you picture yourself as your most perfect image of accomplishment? How does it feel? If you have the desire to attain goals, the commitment to follow through and the ability to creatively imagine yourself in the position you dream of, you are more than halfway there.

The most successful leaders and artists throughout history have followed specific paths and attained their hearts desires. Keep an open mind and a hopeful outlook --then change your thinking. Put on the clothes of success. Act as though you already have accomplished your desires. Then let the reality catch up.

WHAT DO YOU WANT?

Take a choice: Money, Health, Physical Energy, Beauty, Creativity, Recognition, Power, Adventure, Contentment, Achievement, Self-Expression, Authority, Love, Peace of Mind, Enlightenment. Would you like any of these? If you are like most people today, you probably want ALL of these.

But if you search your true desires, you might find that there are a few things you want more than others. And if you keep going in your search, you'll find one desire that has been with you your whole lifetime and is the one path you need to follow.

Although money is the obvious desire, it is usually not the final goal. Indeed, money can, and does buy happiness --up to a point. Once you have enough money to be financially secure or to purchase the material objects you want, the true desire might be something else.

Love is the goal of every person's heart. Whether it is love of a mate, or a family, or respect and recognition from peers and fellow workers, love is the ageless pursuit. The mystics say that love is the sole purpose of life -- to give love and to find it.

But love comes in many forms. Not only is there the overt display of affection or true inner feelings, but there is the self-respect and inner contentment that goes with accomplishment. For some people, true peace of mind will never be attained until they complete some creative tasks or achieve certain heights in business.

Many people seek the authority that comes with a good position in a job. Along with that can come recognition and fame. Although you may want the money that is associated with high management levels, many people simply seek the satisfaction of working from the inner circles.

The goal of every person, regardless of background and material desires, is health. A sound body is the gift that will get you to the other goals. Even a new diet and exercise plan can give you more energy -- the energy you'll need to accomplish success.

Adventure and travel is a driving force for many people. They may seek jobs that involve travel, or they may be looking forward to taking time off to visit the exotic ports and see the other side of the world. If you don't want a long journey, perhaps you'd just like few weeks in a sunny resort, or the luxury of a summer and winter vacation each year.

And then there is creativity and self-expression. What about the book you're going to write or the watercolor class you'd like to take? Creative expression is a wonderful inner release that boosts confidence and gives you something to accomplish.

Finally, regardless of wealth and health, expression and love, everyone is looking for peace of mind. That's not to say emptiness of mind, but to be rid of petty worries and confusion, to be finished with fears and live in total awareness. It surely is the ultimate lifetime goal.

Catch Up With Yourself

NOW's the time to evaluate your life and your desires. Go ahead and test yourself -- nobody's looking. Try to find out what your inner desires really are. Once you know, you can formulate a plan of action, and then achieve your goals.

Right now, write down three things you really want. Don't spend time thinking about them -- just write them down. You may be surprised at what you want. Can you see any relation to the types of desires most sought for?

What accomplishments are you most proud of? What makes you happy -- happy enough to be content, to feel totally relaxed, and to slide back with a smile on your face.

Without dwelling on failures, mistakes, or past ill feelings, quickly list the important accomplishments of your life. Think about the places you went to, the relationships you encountered, the education you received. Consider your job changes and positions, and the achievements related to work.

Put a star next to the most important accomplishments of your life. Is there any correlation with the list of the three things you want most?

Make Plans

Before you go any further with your life, make a list for your future. Write it down -- don't just think it. What would you like to accomplish in the next ten years? A new house, a high-paying position, a home in a new city, a trip around the world?

236

Break that list down into those things you'd like to accomplish in the next five years. Then make one further division into the next six months. What can you do in the next few months to further you towards your long-term goals?

Regardless of your family commitments or your personal relationships; regardless of your business enterprises or any false sense of achievement, what do you really want?

Goal Sheet

My most important desires are:

1._____

_____

_____

2._____

_____

_____

3._____

_____

In my lifetime, the most important things I've accomplished:

_____

_____

_____

_____

_____

_____

_____

_____

If I looked back on my lifetime 20 years from now, I'd like to have accomplished:

_____

_____

_____

_____

_____

_____

_____

Within 10 years, I'd like to achieve: _____

_____

_____

_____

_____

Within 5 years, I'd like to achieve:_____

_____

_____

_____

_____

_____

In the next 6 months to a year, these are the things I'm going to do to work towards my goals:_____

_____

_____

_____

_____

RELIVE THE FUTURE ©

GOAL STATEMENT: (Written in present tense, time-specific,
                    measurable and result-oriented)

SENSORY DESCRIPTION: (What will the goal look, sound, feel,
                    taste and smell like when it is
                    achieved and the emotions you will
                    experience in the surroundings upon
                    completion of your goal)

SIGHT:

SOUND:

FEEL:

TASTE:

SMELL:

EMOTION:

CONSEQUENCES: (WIIFM - What's In It For Me! The benefits or
pay-off you will receive as a result
of achieving your goal)

Always keep focused on your goal by asking yourself this question: "What's more important - my goal or others' opinion of my goal?"

Give yourself credit for your past accomplishments, and give yourself credit for your future achievements. You can and will attain all your goals, both long-term and short-term if you approach them is a step-by-step fashion and if you believe that they are worthwhile for you.

You
Are
Important!

**The purpose of our lives
is to give birth to the best
which is within us.
- Marianne Williamson**

YOU ARE THE MOST IMPORTANT PERSON IN YOUR LIFE.

Although you can be considerate of your environment and all the people in it, first consider yourself - your well-being, your happiness, your success. Make a pact with yourself right now that will achieve your goals. And make them realistic to reach. Then one-by-one, make your own life the success it deserves.

Before the Race -- Relax

An important step in achieving goals is to be able to relax. You'll get nowhere if your body and mind are nervous and flitty, jumping from one place or idea to another. In order to focus on your goal, you must center your being.

Relaxation is the balance of the mental, spiritual and physical aspects of yourself. Set aside time each day for deep relaxation -- not sleep, but relaxation. The state of deep relaxation is a state of meditation. There are no thoughts in your mind. There are no physical ills or discomforts. You breathe in deeply, allowing the lungs to fill with fresh air, and you exhale all used and stale air. The blood circulates amply throughout every part of your body. You drift through space, ever towards your true destiny.

Exercise or sports is a good way to get into relaxation. The body needs physical stimulation to pump blood into all its extremities, and to give the heart a good workout. Exercise is a wonderful way to let the mind relax, as you place your thoughts on the way your body moves. For many people, sports and exercise are enjoyable ways to feel alive, youthful and fulfilled.

Then take the time to relax. Lie down on your back with your arms out, palms up. Your feet should be about two feet apart. You might clench your muscles first, then relax them. Allow your thoughts to drift, but don't get caught in them. Watch them go by, as if they belong to somebody else.

If you have a special problem, tuck that in the back of your mind -- don't dwell on it up front. Let yourself and your emotions go. Breathe out the negative feelings and emotions; breathe in positive, life-giving air. Float freely. Relax.

Assume the Best

Expect to achieve; expect to accomplish your desires; expect to win. Accept less, but push on to attain more. The higher your goals, the further you'll go.

The moon is no problem, nor are the neighboring planets. Soon human beings will see close-ups of other stars and galaxies. Don't go for less than your full potential. Shoot for the universe. You owe yourself nothing less.

And aside from the universe, keep yourself on earth, in your office. studio or home, working closer to those goals you want to attain.

You have a right to be happy. You have the means to be successful. <u>You can succeed in what you desire.</u>

Always keep in mind the fact that you are in transit, attaining your goals, moving through life as though you are an actor, and the setting is a stage.

Keep your thoughts firmly planted on prosperity, good fortune and lucky breaks. Assume that you will -- in fact, nearly have -- accomplished your goals. It is with that attitude that successful people achieve.

Do You Have The Potential?

Within you is the power to accomplish anything you want. But it will not happen if you are not tuned into your true desires.

Don't fool yourself into compromising for less than a complete goal. If you want to be an artist, you may not be the world's most famous artist, but if you have that inclination, you will be an artist. If you want to succeed in business, you may not be another financier/mega-millionaire, but you will succeed in your endeavors.

Most people need accomplishment feedback. After all, what's so great about achieving something if nobody cares? And it's important to receive that recognition and feel that love.

Set goals that you can achieve. Divide them into little tidbits that you can accomplish every day, every month, every year. Set your goals for success.

Then reap the rewards constantly -- each step of the way. Pat yourself on the back for a good job well done, then move on.

Start immediately to accomplish the goals you have set. In fact, give yourself a task that you can finish by tomorrow. Think of yourself as a success in your endeavors. Dwell on the idea that you are compelled to accomplish your goals, and live and breathe them until you have them.

Can you see yourself a year from now, having achieved a few goals? Can you make the decision and commitment to become successful in your desires? Then you have the potential to accomplish anything you want!

The Power Of Self-Image

Visualizing yourself as a success in your field of endeavor is the inside tip in accomplishing anything you want. If you can specifically imagine being the person you want to become, you will attain that reality.

Forgive yourself. Just as you would another person, tell yourself that it's okay for all those mistakes, or the should-haves that keep popping up in your mind. Don't dwell on the past and get blocked by events from long ago.

Let go of fears and anxieties. Although it certainly is easier said than done, learn to change negative thoughts into a positive action. Are you afraid of poverty -- that you'll never make ends meet, or never buy that house, or be destitute once you stop working? Then turn that into the goal of financial security.

Do people make you anxious? Maybe you feel inferior, not as good as others. Everybody has feeling of inadequacy. Just turn them around into positive goals. You may be paralyzed by the thoughts that you are unattractive. It is your thoughts that make it a reality. Change your modes of behavior and you will make friends.

In most cases, it is your negative thoughts that cause you to stay stuck in whatever place you're in. Keep moving. Take the risks. You may need to change your job, or move to another city. You might take up a sport or hobby. Become active in your life -- participate. And you will grow into the image you see of yourself.

Succeed In Business

Perhaps the most sought-after goal in our present society is success in business. Whether you want to be promoted into high-paying management positions, or wish to start your own independent enterprise, knowledge of the business world is important.

As you plan a course of action towards accomplishing your goal, keep in mind the small goals that put you closer to the end. And be prepared to change often. You may need to change companies, or take the opportunities in other departments as those positions open.

Create an aura of success around you. People who are successful dress that way. Even if you're not in a high-income bracket, act as though you have already achieved -- without being egotistical or overspending.

Develop an expertise in an area. Don't keep special

information to yourself, but be quick to learn all there is about your position and the tasks surrounding getting that job done. Capitalize on your strengths, and let others help you develop your weaknesses into assets.

Get to know the people in the company and the people in the industry. Read all the trade journals and magazines relating to your company. Make appointments with people who are successful in your field and learn from them.

You need to have a total commitment to succeed in business. Most people who make it to the executive boardroom put in long hours, often at the sacrifice of everything else. Regardless of the physical effort involved, you must mentally be engrossed in your business and the company enterprises.

In order to help yourself develop fully, you might seek a mentor, someone who will offer you time and teach you the ropes. This person usually is someone who believes in your ability, someone who you can develop a mutually beneficial business relationship with.

Some people become friendly with all their co-workers and find that is a way to advance. But don't try to be extroverted if it's not real to you. Most people who successfully run their own businesses are individuals who like to work alone.

As you increase your activities and accomplishments, you increase your potential to reach higher. The more you achieve, the more confidence you develop to achieve more.

You don't have to be the same as everyone else and fit like a vegetable in a patch. Be unique, different. Capitalize on your self-image. Don't fall victim to self-consciousness. And trust your intuition. Hunches and inner feelings usually are the best routes to travel, regardless of what seems to be the logical choice.

Make decisions quickly and with firmness. A true leader will handle these responsibilities efficiently. That's what makes you different and why you'll rise to the top.

Be persistent in attaining your goals, but be open and sincere. Many people choose not to increase their own accomplishments and will give you the right-of-way to be successful.

If you are having personal difficulties with any co-workers, try to know more about these people from a personal angle. Be interested in them and their accomplishments and goals. You might be able to turn opposition into friendship.

Above all, use your integrity. If the goal is not worthy of your inner desires, it will be hard to attain. If your methods are not sincere, you will receive opposition. If your actions are not honest, you will suffer the consequences. Turn all negative aspects into positive qualities -- then watch yourself achieve.

Tips On Attaining Wealth

Many people want money as a primary goal. And there certainly is nothing wrong with desiring money. But first, be sure that your true goal is money. Can you live, breathe, eat, and sleep money? Do you dream about money and want it more than anything?

For true money-seekers, you must be your own boss. The great money-makers all started and ran their own businesses. And, even though it seems as though all the good ideas have already been taken, there are plenty out there.

The secret of the wealthiest people is to find a special need and fill it. Like quick-food chains; like supermarkets; like electronic games. Whether you invent a new toy or gadget, or see a spot to market special items in a new way, the world is open to true entrepreneurs. And they do make it.

Learn Your Trade

Almost any goal you choose -- whether riches and material

abundance or spiritual attainment -- requires learning. How much education do you have? Do you want more? Perhaps your goal is to get another degree or to secure a special license.

There are countless opportunities to learn more about your own industry or to learn about a new skill. Not only do you have the colleges and universities, but there are many trade schools, correspondence schools, and special groups that teach skills -- at very reasonable prices.

Keep the end in mind. What do you need to know to get to where you want to be? You may not need a degree, but the actual experience. So you'd need to change jobs or accept a part-time job at night to develop your skills.

More than ever, people are leaving their present occupations to learn a new trade and then starting at the bottom again to be happy in their work. Maybe you'll need to put in extra hours at work now so you can save money to take the time off next year.

Even though most entry-level positions are offered to the younger people, you can find many companies willing to give you a chance to change your occupation. Many times you might find an older master willing to apprentice you to learn the skill or trade.

Once you're enrolled to learn new skills, put everything towards learning. Apply yourself one hundred percent. Take advantage of asking questions and getting criticism from teachers and associate students. Read everything you can and study well. It is your developing expertise that will get you ahead and closer to your goal.

Anytime is a good time to learn more. Even if you're happy in your job, expanding yourself through education is a very rewarding activity. Take dancing or tennis, gourmet cooking or sculpture. Take a comedy class or join Toastmasters International. Almost any activity is taught and usually has a group of enthusiastic, sharing people.

Stop Wasting Time

Consider the most important things you need to accomplish. These are the high priorities. Then think about those things that seem to take up a lot of time and get you nowhere. Those are the low priorities.

Understand what's important to achieve and do those things first. Let go of all the busywork or paperwork that piles up. It's better for you to stack those low priorities somewhere else and finish the important material than to spend time clearing your desk to get down to the essential things.

You'll be noticed quicker for the big things you achieve than for keeping paper flowing. Don't let co-workers waste your time with chit-chat if you've got things to accomplish. Save that for lunch hours or for after work social activities.

Handle paper once; decide the action and finish with it. Keep interruptions to a minimum. Delegate responsibilities. Although you'd like to believe you're indispensable to the job and you are the only one to take care of things, you can teach someone else and move on to your own goal achievement.

Don't procrastinate. What are you waiting for? Few opportunities are thrown at you; you have to create the right positions and situations to move up. Make lists of things you want to accomplish and do them!

If you're busy in an office situation, make daily lists and reward yourself with praise upon completion. Catch yourself achieving.

Concentrate on what you're doing and do one thing at a time. But do it quickly and handle the next thing. Be efficient in telephone calls, maybe taking them at appointed times or calling back at your convenience.

Don't generate copies or correspondence just to make it look like you doing something. Your superiors will know what you accomplish. Be busy doing important things rather than writing about what you've done.

And take the time for physical exercise. It will energize you -- not take away from your effectiveness. It relaxes your mind and stimulates your capacity to achieve.

Look Within

In the inner core of all accomplishments is the positive energy from the subconscious. If your subconscious mind has tapped into your goal and believes it is good for you, your energies will direct themselves towards that goal.

You can consciously create circumstances and conditions of environment and physical presence. But it is that level behind the outwardly physical that directs your true being. When the subconscious mind accepts and idea, the inner power will complete it.

That's why you can accomplish anything you want -- by creating all outward manifestations to trigger your subconscious into action. As you decide on your goals and write them down, repeat them twice a day out loud. This in essence brings it to the inner level.

When you think about your goals and desires, the subconscious hears it. So direct you energies -- both outer and inner -- to your goal with one-pointed devotion. In that way, you can control your destiny.

In order to connect to your inner self, relax -- let your thoughts go. Feel that part within you that actually makes the decisions -- the reflexes, the instincts, the intuition and hunches. Let your mind be quiet from its usual chatter.

Some people present problems to their inner conscious-ness by asking themselves a question before they fall asleep. Often the answer is in their minds when they wake up.

Clarity rids confusion. If you find you're filled with worries and anxieties, spend the time to think them through. Approach them logically, considering the consequences of all possible actions. When you've made a decision, follow through and don't agonize over 'what-ifs'.

Everybody has creative potential. And you don't have to be an artist to be creative. Each moment of the day is creating your own self, becoming your true inner person.

Let yourself look within. Release the handicaps of fear and anxiety -- even for a moment. You'll be relaxed and refreshed.

Use Affirmations

The same technique has been used by great inventors, financiers, business people, political figures, athletes, and enlightened beings; constant repetition of the goal and the belief that you can attain it.

Never dwell on self-criticism or what you think are your inadequacies. Instead, repeat your goals and the qualities that will make you successful.

Write out your outstanding goal. In a few words, describe what you want to attain. Then write what you will do to achieve that. What energies and efforts will you trade for that success?

Give yourself a specific date to accomplish this goal, and specific times to carry out the interim steps. Put this paper or notecard in a visible place -- such as taped to the mirror -- so you can review it and repeat it at least twice a day.

It is those people who convince themselves that they are failures who become failures. And successful people believe that they will rise to the top and will achieve their goals. Believe in yourself. You are everything worth believing in.

Creative Visualization

Form the habit of accomplishment. With every step you take and every decision you make, bring yourself closer to your goals. Walk through your life with this sense of direction and it will come to you.

Develop self-confidence and esteem. Assert yourself and acquire all the excellent qualities and traits you admire most.

What is your ultimate goal? How do you see yourself? Be specific. Precisely specific. Visualize the place you live in -- the rooms, the paintings on the walls, the furniture and swimming pool. Consider the family situation and financial stability. Think about the place you'll be living in.

Then look at yourself. What clothes are you wearing and what do you look like? Consider your physique, your hair, the condition of your body.

Then think about the things you do. What sports do you play, what groups do you belong to?

As if you've already accomplished your desires, look back and see what you did to get to where you are. Think about the classes you took, the jobs you worked at, and the places you moved to. Think about the places you've traveled to and the friends you've made.

Be comfortable with your new self-image. Put it on for size and change your fantasy to adjust perfectly to you. Why don't you look as though you're already there? What's stopping you from becoming the person you are totally capable of becoming?

Become Your Full Potential

Keep your goals and ambitions to yourself -- don't share them with anyone, not yet. Write them down and refer to them. Look back at what you wrote in a month, then in a few months. Work on them constantly, and don't be afraid to revise and rewrite. Goals are always changing.

Think in possibilities. What is possible for you to achieve in the next six months? And go for it. Don't play it safe with what you'll probably achieve anyway. Push yourself to go further. The rewards are greater.

Feel the winning feeling. Feel successful already. Try on the clothes of total accomplishment and peace of mind. Live each day as though you have already reached your goals. There are always new ones to place in front of yourself.

Don't announce your goals. This will set you up for failure. Even if you make a pact with yourself to attain a specific goal, don't chastise yourself if you don't make it. It may have been unrealistic or you may not have tried hard enough.

Do it yourself. There is nobody better to help you achieve your desires than you. Tap into the power of the subconscious and practice being your own fantasy.

Go ahead. Act on your convictions. Follow them through with devotion and then reap the rewards. You CAN accomplish anything you want in life.

HAVE A FANTASTIC LIFE AND MAKE EVERY HOUR - HAPPY HOUR - IN YOUR LIFE!!!